MOVE YOUR MOUNTAINS

Learn the Journey of
FAITH
that Can Overcome

Macil Duncan

Copyright © 2023

Move Your Mountains
Learn the Journey of FAITH that Can Overcome
Macil Duncan

ISBN: 978-1-944265-64-9

FIRST EDITION

The views and opinions expressed in this book are the sole expression and opinion of the author, which is based on the personal and practical experience of the author on the matters contained within this book and does not necessarily reflect the opinion, position or views of Foresight Book Publishing Co., which does not endorse or warranty any claims expressed by the author or contained within this book.

All rights reserved. This book is protected by the copyright laws of the United States of America. This book may not be copied or reprinted for commercial gain or profit. Permission will be granted upon request. No part of this book may be reproduced without written permission, except for brief quotations in books and critical reviews.

For information, contact
Foresight Book Publishing
Chattanooga, TN 37419

FORESIGHT BOOK PUBLISHING
ForesightPublishingNow.com
Info@ForesightPublishingNow.com

"Scripture taken from the NEW AMERICAN STANDARD BIBLE,
Copyright © 1960, 1962, 1963 1968, 1971, 1972,
1973 1975, 1977, 1995 by The Lockman Foundation
All rights reserved
Used by permission.
http://www.Lockman.org

Table of Contents

Dedication	7
Acknowledgment	9
Introduction	11
Running on Empty Faith	11
Section I: The Journey of Faith	15
Chapter : Defining Genuine Faith	17
Chapter 2: How's Your Soil?	27
Chapter 3: Moving Mountains by Faith	39
Section I Summary: The Journey of Faith	51
Section II: Moving the Mountain of Bitterness	51
Chapter 4: The Overcoming Power of Forgiveness	53
Chapter 5: The 12-Hour Anger Limit	63
Chapter 6: Healing Through Faith Conflicts	73
Section II Summary: How to Move the Mountain of Bitterness	81
Section III: Dealing with the Mountain of Division	83
Chapter 7: Faith Fixing Solutions	85
Chapter 8: How Not to Stumble	93
Chapter 9: Serve and Overcome	101
Section III Summary: Dealing with the Mountain of Division	109
Section IV: Conquering the Mountain of Fear	111
Chapter 10: Fear Lies	113
Chapter 11: Following Jesus in the Midst of Fear	123
Chapter 12: Faith Is Fueled by Provision	131
Section IV Summary: Conquering the Mountain of Fear	143
Epilogue: Love Is the Destination	145
About the Author	149
Authors' Point of Contact	151
Endnotes	153

DEDICATION

*To my wife, Judy, who is my best friend,
partner, and prayer warrior.*

*To my parents, Claude and Barbara Duncan, whose
faith raised me up so that I could walk and live by faith.*

*To my beloved three daughters and their husbands.
Shaina and Micah; Rachel and Issiah; Maci and Joe.*

*Your continued support and encouragement to
step out in faith has been such a blessing.*

ACKNOWLEDGMENT

This book has been the effort of many years of journaling, where I poured out my heart to God, highlighting my heart's desires, hurts, triumphs, and the overcoming of hard-fought battles for His glory. I have been privileged to have a front-row-seat to God's glorious unfolding plan throughout all my life. My prayer is that you'll be encouraged in your walk of faith as you read this book.

While I could fill a chapter, and some are noted within chapters in this book, I'd like to share my appreciation to several who have made this journey all the more richer.

My sister Michelle and her husband Chris for your continued prayers and support throughout all areas of my life.

Special friends that have supported my ministry: Rev. Doug Hinshaw, Susan Foster, Cheri Taylor, Roy & Darla Lemons, Rick & Kim Patterson, Terry Rowe, Dan & Rhonda Martin, Merrel Hampton, Paul Wardlaw, Lynn Davis, Ginny Nowell, Dr. PJ & Betty Scott, Dr. Johnny Hunt, Bill & Linda Hullander, Matt Hullander, Walt and Jill Model, Senator Todd Gardenhire, Congressman Chuck Fleischmann, State Representative Greg Vital, Dr. Rick Scarbough VISION AMERICA, Dr. Steve Rumley (R.I.P.), Jimmy & Kim Vincent Jr, Mayor Jim & Maryln Vincent, TN Baptist leader Steve Pearson, fellow radio host David Tullis, radio owners Tim & Sab, David Bandy, MOMs for America Maria Wager, Joleen Carter, Bobby Parker, Josh Kilgore.

The Apison Food Pantry leadership and friends: Executive board members: Janet, Linda, Mary, Imogene, Jill, and Judy on the executive. To Church leaders: Ralph & Lisa, Caroline, Leon, Richard & Charlotte, Betty, Matt & Lindsey. To Annette, who originally asked me to serve at the Pantry. To Charlene, who joined our church because of the pantry. And to the church family at Apison

Baptist, these past six years of your prayers and support of the ministry. To Chuck Wallace, with Campus Crusade for Christ, who discipled me in high school. And so many others that invested in me on many levels and across so many years in my walk with Christ.

The Lord called me into ministry at age thirteen. Fast forward and it's now been 45 years of serving the Lord. Over this time, I have served as a Youth & Family Minister, full time Evangelist & Conference Speaker, Senior Pastor, started a non-profit called CHAMPIONSHIP MINISTRIES Inc to help raise funds for bibles, materials, ministry projects, camps, and conferences.

This book is one of many I plan on writing to encourage and help inspire others in their faith journey.

INTRODUCTION

Running on Empty Faith

My father gave me his 1972 Volkswagen Super Beatle with the full Rolls Royce kit a few years ago. I park it in the winter months, and then each spring and summer I drive it until early fall arrives. This past year as I went to start, "The Song Bug," as my father calls it, the engine would not turn over. No problem. I was prepared. I got out the battery trickle down charger and hooked it up for 24 hours.

24 hours later… it still would not start. At this point, I decided I was in over my head, so I called a member of my church to come help me. His name is Walter, and as an international airline pilot and show car enthusiast, he knows his way around an engine. He is an engineer, operator, and grease monkey all rolled into one. We call him "Buzz Lightyear." Now, finally, we would be able to figure out what was wrong with my car.

Buzz and I began to do procedures and tests, but nothing came up. We did a couple of tricks he had learned over the years to help get the carburetor clear, we checked the fire pins, the spark plugs, but after hours, Buzz packed up his tools in defeat and said he could not fix it. He owns seven show cars and is very experienced with engines. If Buzz was confused, then it must be sad news. He is like MacGyver fixing things. I decided to call a specialist as a last, desperate attempt. I told him that he had better bring his trailer, because he would probably have to take it back to the shop with him to completely overhaul the engine.

The next day, the VW Mechanic came to the house, and within 15 minutes he said he had diagnosed the problem.

"Great!" I said. "What's going on with this thing?"

He said, "Preacher, you do know this is a combustion engine?"

I said yes. "Did you not know," he continued, "that combustion engines need gasoline for the engine to run?"

I could not believe it! Something so simple, and here I was treating the car like it needed a team of nuclear physicists to fix it.

Humiliated, I went to the shed, got some gas, and poured it in. The Song Bug started right up.

Now, I know a lot of you are reading this snickering now, and thinking, "What a dummy." Fair enough, I did not have my head on straight that day. But we have all done something like this. I have a friend who called his wife to ask him where his phone was. He had looked "everywhere." Everywhere, except in his hand.

Sometimes the answer is right there in front of you, and sometimes the car just needs gas.

We all do this from time to time – We look urgently at the symptoms of our problem when something is not working, but in the midst of being so concerned, we don't check our fuel source. And everything has a fuel source.

For cars, it is gasoline. For your phone, it is electricity. For your body, it is food.

But what is your fuel for life?

Life is made up of a lot of different things: relationships, work, rest, decisions, purpose and meaning, etc. So, what is fueling you as you go through all of it?

Not all sources of fuel are created equal. If I put unleaded in my Song Bug, it will run, but if I use super premium, it'll hum like a dream. If I put sugar in the gas tank, it will not run at all – now or ever again!

Your body is the same way. You can live off Twinkies and Coca Cola, at least for a while, but a balanced, healthy diet is going to save you a literal headache and a whole lot else that is worse.

Your soul needs fuel for life, and what is more it needs good fuel.

God's Word is the best source of fuel you can find for your soul. It is the best thing you can fill up with to send you out, ready to grapple with the issues of life. When we go days, months or even years without talking to God or reading the scriptures, it just is not that surprising that we aren't moving forward with our faith – and more likely than not, we're also feeling some depression, conflict in our relationships, and uncertainty... EMPTY!

Many people, just like "The Song Bug," are empty for the journey. Now, that VW had already traveled miles and miles over the years, and if those doors and wheels could talk, you can imagine the adventures the old car could tell. But it still could not start up and drive out of the garage without fresh fuel. The past is good to remember, but we cannot hang up our cleats. We have to move forward into the future.

Psalm 119 is the longest chapter in the bible with many great quotes about the importance of God's Word, like, "It is a lamp unto my feet and light to my path."[1] It also teaches that we are to hide Gods Word in our hearts that we might not sin against Him. That means it is not just reading but applying lessons and guidance for life. To hide is not to conceal it; it is to implant the Word so deeply in our souls, that it inspires us daily.

As a boy, I would look down the hallway into the mirror in my parents' room and watch my father read his bible every night. I wanted to be like my dad, so I would read my bible every night, too. I would turn a page when he did, and I learned not just the message but a life pattern of daily searching the Bible for wisdom. It impacted my faith and reminded me to keep my heart full of scripture for the rough roads ahead.

We are left now with this question: how do we discover a faith that can move mountains?

Jesus tells us and invites us to join Him on this journey, turn the page, and read on.

SECTION I

The Journey of Faith

Chapter 1

Defining Genuine Faith

Now I grew up in a Christian home, so my parents taught me to have faith even for the unimportant things in life and that God would provide. At age 13, I was called to ministry, and shortly after that, a minister challenged us kids to make a list of things we wanted in our future spouses and to pray for them every day until we met them. I was 20 years old went I met Judy so for seven years I prayed for her daily, (mind you I was in Junior High).

1. That she would be a faithful Christian woman
2. That she would want to be a minister's wife and partner with me in helping others know God
3. That she was a blonde
4. That she was a cheerleader (stop laughing)
5. That she would not scare me in the morning with no makeup
6. That she would want to have children
7. That she would be my best friend and prayer partner
8. That she would be a helper to the ministry
9. That she could forgive me when I failed
10. That she would follow me wherever God led us

God answered my top ten and much more. My parents shared with me that they had been praying for my spouse since my conception.

Pray for God to give your child a heart to know and follow Him.
 −Jeremiah 24:7

Pray for God's protection and watchfulness over your child's steps.
 − Psalm 121:3

Judy, my wife, had siblings that rode the bus to church as kids. If she missed the bus, a lady in the community would pick her up for service on Sundays. Judy in her college young adult days was a bus captain and helped plan routes for kids to be able to attend church that needed a ride as well. She had a ministry calling and passion for Christ. Even though we had not met I was praying for her all that time.

Today, Judy tells me she believes it was the faithful prayers of my parents and my prayers for her. She is my best friend and prayer partner, and our faith adventure in ministry with our three daughters has been one only God could have designed. We have three daughters, Shaina, Rachel and Maci, and we prayed for them from conception through to this day.

Pray for God's mercy and righteousness to be upon your child and their descendants.
 − Psalm 103:17

Praying in faith for your spouse, your children are very personal parts of our life, and we must pray believing He hears every word.

Do you have faith for the moment, the season or even better for your life to be in the hands of an almighty loving God? Can you – without doubt – know that He loves you with a plan, even when things look disturbing or bleak?

Let me tell you a story.

When Hudson Taylor was sailing to China to begin his missionary work, his ship fell into great danger. The wind died and refused to pick up again, and in those days, no wind meant that you were at the mercy of the currents. That wasn't always too big a deal, but in this case, the current was carrying them toward sunken reefs, which could tear the hull of their ship to bits. And even if they missed the reefs, the current was also pulling them towards islands inhabited by cannibals—they were so close that they could actually see them building fires on the shore.

They were facing either death by drowning or murder by cannibals. The wind stubbornly refused to fill their sails, and the weather was not promising any change. In parts of the Pacific Ocean, such as where they were, it could be days before there would be any wind again.

So, they tried everything they could think of – Could they row the ship? No, it was too big. Could they get creative with the sails to catch anything in them. No, there was not even a breeze.

Nothing was working, and they were out of options. Time was literally running out.

> *In his journal, Taylor recorded what happened next:*
>
> *The captain said to me, "Well, we have done everything that can be done."*
>
> *A thought occurred to me, and I replied, "No, there is one thing we have not done yet."*
>
> *"What is that?" he queried.*
>
> *"Four of us on board are Christians. Let us each retire to his own cabin, and in agreed prayer ask the Lord to give us immediately a breeze."*

Taylor prayed briefly, and then, certain that the answer was coming, went up on the deck and asked the first officer to let down the sails.

> *"What would be the good of that?" he answered roughly. I told him we had been asking a wind from God; that it was coming immediately.*

Within minutes, the wind began to blow, and it carried them safely past the reefs. Taylor wrote:

> *Thus, God encouraged me ere landing on China's shores to bring every variety of need to Him in prayer, and to expect that He would honor [sic] the name of the Lord Jesus and give the help each emergency required.*

That is faith.

The Epistle to the Hebrews in the Bible puts it this way:

> *Now faith is the certainty of things hoped for, a proof of things not seen.*
>
> – Hebrews 11:1

Some translations say "substance" instead of "certainty" in that verse because the Greek word does not necessarily mean something subjective. It is not that you are certain, it is that it is certain.

Faith is more than pie in the sky, good thoughts, and vibes. Faith is a force. Faith is real.

But for a lot of people, there is a big gap between what they tell you they believe in and how they live their lives. Today, we would say that's the difference between belief and faith. Belief is just thoughts in your head, and faith is what you act on.

I can believe that this chair in front of my computer is going to hold me up if I sit in it, but if I get flimsy with you about actually sitting in it, then I don't really have faith in it, no matter what I say that I think.

James puts it this way:

> *You believe that God is one. You do well; the demons also believe, and shudder.*
>
> – James 2:19

James has a way with words, doesn't he? He tells it like it is.

A lot of people say that they are Christians, or that they believe in Jesus.

You might not expect to hear this from a preacher such as myself, but to that I say, "So what?"

> *Not everyone who says to me, "Lord, Lord," will enter the kingdom of heaven, but the one who does the will of my Father who is in heaven will enter.*
>
> – Matthew 7:21

The demons believe there is a God. More than believe it – they know it! And it terrifies them. But they do not submit to God. They are not on His team. They are not letting Him be their guiding force.

They are in rebellion, doing things on their own terms.

It is not going to work out so well for them, by the way.

We talk about faith like it means "belief" or "what I'd sign on a doctrinal statement." But we should talk about faith more in terms of "trust."

Put your money where your mouth is, you might say.

"Why is my faith being tested?" folks often say during demanding times. The answer is that it would not be faithful if it hadn't been tested. Faith is that which is evaluated. It is the assurance of what you hope for. It is the evidence of these ideas floating around that you say you believe.

Judy will tell you she had three men propose to marry her. Once we met, dated, and prayed, we both knew we had found not just our soulmates, but answered prayers that took years to come to reality. Faith for the journey is not a Happy Meal with a prize guaranteed in 15 minutes or less. Sometimes we must have faith for long lengths of time, like Abraham did for his promised son or Noah while building the ark. And sometimes, we need short moments of faith in a crisis, like David killing the Giant.

We need to follow Jesus' instructions, and not just get a bumper sticker that says, "The Bible says it; I believe it; that settles that."

Interestingly, in the original language of the Bible, there is not a different word for "faith" and "belief." We differentiate in the English because of how we speak, but in the minds of the writers of the Bible, it seems like when they say "pistis"[2] – the word for faith or belief – they're assuming that what you think in your head is going to dictate what you actually do.

Makes sense, right?

Similarly, the Old Testament word for ""here"" and "obey" are the same.[3] It assumes that if you hear an instruction from God, or from a legitimate authoriy, you will do it.

We ought to be simple like that in our thinking with these questions. I have heard God, so of course I've got to do it. I believe in my head that Jesus is the Messiah, so of course I am going to learn from His teachings and live the life of faith.

So, what is faith? We throw around that word a lot. Wayne Grudem defines saving faith as "Trust in Jesus Christ as a living purpose for forgiveness of sins and eternal life."

Now, that is good, and I believe in that. But here is the problem we've been circling around:

A lot of people want just enough "faith" to stay out of Hell. They do not really want God when you think about it. Sometimes atheists tell Christians that their faith is just "fire insurance," and while I tend not to think much of the arguments from atheists, this is a good critique of a lot of people.

But my faith is not just fire insurance, and I hope yours isn't either. Jesus said to abide in Him. And that means a few different things, but here is what I want to focus on:

Saying that we follow Jesus has implications. It means that when we put our faith in Him, we have got a new way of living, which is different from the way of the flesh, the natural way of doing things without thinking about what God wants.

Jesus called His disciples by saying "Follow Me." He also says, "Forgive them." If you are having trouble with your spouse, we say, "Get a divorce!" Jesus says, "Let not man separate what God has brought together."[4] We say, "Self-love!" Jesus says, "Love others as much as you love yourself." We say, "You can live however you want, get rich quick, and maybe have God on the side." Jesus says, "You can't serve God, and money as a god, at the same time."

I will give you an example, from how I've had to learn to walk this out in my own life.

When I was a young preacher, just out of seminary, I had two paths laid out in front of me: Go to a big, well-funded church and earn a good salary, or go to small, troubled churches where my financial well-being would be an open question.

I served on three exceptionally large church staff that ran multiple services, had large budgets, and big events. Those times were enjoyable, and I logged 18 years as a student minister in Mississippi, Texas, and North Carolina.

When I was on staff at the large churches, we led hundreds of people to Christ and I developed a discipleship program called P.O.W. (Pursuing Our

SECTION I: *The Journey Of Faith*

Witness) that took a student 3 years to complete, which included memorizing scripture, authoring papers on doctrine, learning their spiritual gifts, and then using those gifts in ministry. In 18 years, we launched over thirty students into ministry and missions, trained thousands on how to share their faith, and took these young people into the field to share. Then, on some of our mission trips, I noticed how we would go into a smaller church, help them win souls, facilitate projects, canvas neighborhoods, and it was wonderful. But then we would get back into our buses and head home, leaving the smaller church to walk out their church growth needs solo.

All churches have problems and issues because of humanity's sin nature. In larger churches, due to their size, most issues can be covered up or shadowed by the congregation. In a smaller church, all eyes are on everything all the time, and it forces better communication, more patience, working together, and making finances go further. We had many great victories, some very disappointing moments, and we learned that not everyone who calls themselves a Christian genuinely wants to emulate Christ's teachings.

Jesus said, "It isn't the well that need a doctor, but the sick," so I figured that I had better go where I was needed.

At one church in particular, I took a pay cut to earn the least I have made in a long time, and on paper it just didn't add up. But my wife and the Lord were calling us to serve in that church. We drove down twice and did prayer rides in the community and fasted for God's favor.

Then, my wife's work started offering benefits, so insurance was provided and then, come to find out, the church also provided a parsonage – a house for the preacher and his family to live in. We have always owned our own home and the thought of going to a parsonage is concerning as we are getting older, but we must trust the Lord to provide when the time comes for us to retire.

All the investment and future-planning courses I'd taken were screaming, "Pass on this one!" We were by no means wanting to get wealthy from this assignment, but it seemed like an unnerving financial situation. We realized, however, that we were just now empty nesters, and all three girls had moved into adult life, and it was actually Judy that first said she had peace about going to this church. The church, Apison Baptist was back in my hometown in Chattanooga, Tennessee where I served at age 18 as a Summer Youth Minister to be my first paid ministry position.

God asked us to act in faith, and we did. That faith was real because it was in Him, and He had made it all work out.

This church had experienced multiple splits, to the point where one group led all the youth and youth workers to walk out on a Sunday morning service at Christmas, throwing their keys to the church on the altar as they walked out. The remaining members, strong-rooted faithful, were in for a tough season of sticking together. This is the situation that I entered, as pastor of the relaunch. No young people or young families, wounded members that many told me later had a foot out the door if one more issue happened. Yet God gave me a peace like Gideon, that this little army of faith could do grandiose things if we only had the faith to believe in Him. My wife calls our church "Gideons Army."

My first Sunday I asked the Apison Baptist family this question, "If our church ceased to exist, would the community weep our absence?" All churches large or small should be noticed by the local citizens of faith as well as the unchurched. Our mission was to heal the faithful that remained, fast and pray for our future ministry and let God have control. I led us in fasting, prayer walks, scripture dives and some books on seeking His face. We needed a "Faith Face Lift." We re-did the bylaws, policy procedures, and a new purpose statement after eight open and honest family meetings where I asked the members to be honest about the problems so we could find solutions. We had eight tables with a leader at each table to facilitate short discussions and then I would lead in the large sessions and write on a large board their hearts and feelings. Then I would share scripture regarding the church and what our purpose should be as believers.

In short, Judy and I start our seventh year this August 2023. We have survived COVID, a deadly tornado, and rebuilt the mission of the church and now have a Food Pantry that is open 7 days a week, feeding hundreds weekly. Plus, we take food and supplies to the homeless downtown. God took a broken church that still had faith to re-build to reach more people now than ever.

Our purpose statement is: *"Taking Jesus as He is to people as they are."* Our desire is not to be the biggest church on Sunday in a building; our desire is to be Monday-Sunday church, daily impacting lives in the community.

As a bonus of taking this assignment, I now have a daily radio show that reaches thousands of people each day. God is amazing!

SECTION I: *The Journey Of Faith*

We are supposed to live by faith, not by sight. I have done both in my life, and I'm here to say that living by faith is better.

This does not mean that we do not ever have doubts. But we do not have to be afraid of doubts because God is the one who owns all truth, and digging into our questions usually leads to a deeper understanding. But we also need to take the next step to follow God anyway, even when we are in that process of working out our doubts. Do not let doubt limit your faith.

My brother-in-law Dr Chris Stephens pastors one of the largest churches in Tennessee, Faith Promise. They have led the state in baptism over 12 years in a row.

He battled a big moment of doubt, wondering if he was called into to ministry. That is hard to believe today because Faith Promise and its multiple campuses that run thousands a week in around Knoxville. It all started as a small church plant about 25 years ago with a small group of people.

A friend of mine Anthony was their part time youth minister, he told me they were a new work and needed a pastor, I called Chris and got his resume and sent a cover letter to the search team and the rest as they say is history, Faith Promise owes me one but that's ok.

Chris has only pastored 2 churches, both church plants and he was the founding pastor. I mention that to say at one time when Chris was out of Seminary he went almost a year with no preaching opportunities, no staff positions, and was working construction. He stayed humble, fasting, and praying but he was getting discouraged. Then God sent him to a little church in Louisiana, Bethel Baptist, out in the middle of field that flooded when it rained. He grew that church to purchase property and build a Christian school.

He grew Bethel and Faith Promise. He had a year of no ministry before them that he will tell you defined who he still is today. We all have those ditch digging moments, you seem all alone, like John the Baptist in prison second guessing is Jesus the promised one or should we look for another. At times God wants you all to himself, He is a jealous God. Those 12 months Chris was without a church molded him and humbled him to be the man of God he is today. He has a defined faith based on a *TESTimony*!

Do not be discouraged if your plans or hopes are modified by the Lord. If we trust Him, then all will work out for His glory.

My life verse is Proverbs 3:5-6, for many times I do not understand at first, and then, in time, BINGO it all makes sense.

> *Trust in the Lord with all your heart and do not lean on your own understanding. In all your ways acknowledge Him, and He will make your paths straight.*
> – Proverbs 3:5-6b

Chapter 2

How's Your Soil?

My daddy grew up in the country and was taught how to "homestead," as we call it today. He grew up hunting, fishing, and growing veggies, which brought him a lot of joy. As a young boy, I watched my father plant and tend to his garden, and he would teach me life lessons that I still use to this day. He would teach me about gardening, how to work the soil, prepare for the seed, weed the garden before and during the life cycle of the seed, and then how to pick the vegetables at the right time. He also would talk about the seasons for planting and picking what was sown.

One time he held a seed and told me, "Macil, there is life in this little thing. As we plant it into the earth and tend to it, it will grow, and once picked, it will provide food for us to have life." Then he reminded me of the Garden of Eden story, that because of the original sin, man had to work for his food. There is life in the seed, but there are elements in the soil we must take care of so that the life in the seed can grow.

Seeds are important when you think about it.

In fact, deep in the remote, frozen tundra of Norway, just eight hundred miles from the North Pole, lies a guarded facility. This highly secure location is buried 430 feet deep in the side of a mountain plateau, kept precisely at 0 degrees Fahrenheit, and locked behind a series of vault doors.

The security system is highly sophisticated, in which there is only a single key code for each vault door. The contents of the remotest vault are considered so valuable that everything is redundant – even a backup chilling system is in place to ensure that it always stays at the proper temperature.

This vault is said to be able to withstand extreme climate change, natural disasters, acts of war, or even a cataclysmic event. The treasure inside is so well protected that even if the planet's weather shifted drastically and all the electricity failed, the airtight, heavily insulated final room inside of the vault would remain properly frozen for 200 years.

Amazing, right?

"So, what's inside?" you are probably asking. "And why are you talking about a high-tech installation all of the sudden after talking about tending plants?"

It is because this multimillion-dollar, multinational effort is not housing military secrets.

It is not preserving bigfoot, the Loch Ness monster, or the remains of an alien UFO crash.

It is not to protect a secret wormhole, time machine, or quantum leap technology.

What so much time, effort, money, and thought has come together to protect is something much simpler, even fundamental.

This facility houses seeds.

Yes, you read that right. Seeds. Six million samples of seeds, from all across the world.

It is easy, insulated as we are by screens, telecommunications, and all kinds of technology, to forget that everything we eat still comes from a plant or an animal that eats those plants. The survival of our entire species depends on plants reproducing year after year.

And only one little seed can grow into a plant that yields food and thousands of additional seeds.

It truly is miraculous.

But here is the thing – for seeds to do their thing, they need the proper conditions. If you do not believe me, try mixing up a bag of concrete and tossing a few sunflower seeds in it, and see if they grow. But do not hold your breath, if you try this little science experiment.

So, what does this have to do with faith?

There is a parallel between the natural laws we observe in the world and the spiritual laws we experience in our hearts and in our lives.

In nature:

The seed needs soil to hide in, to nourish it, and to anchor it.

In the spirit:

The Word of God can grow in hearts, but only if that heart is able to hide it, live it, and give it a place to flourish.

We are like the soil. Faith is like a seed. God is like a gardener.

Does that surprise you to hear God described this way? We tend to think of thunder and lightning when we think of God, and for good reason! God is powerful. But he is also a careful gardener, fostering life and growing things in brilliant order.

This is what Jesus teaches and it lays a foundation for us to be able to live a life of faith at all. Because one of the first questions we ever need to ask ourselves on this journey is, "What kind of soil am I?"

> *And [Jesus] told them many things in parables, saying, "Behold, the sower went out to sow; and as he sowed, some seeds fell beside the road, and the birds came and ate them up. Others fell on the rocky places, where they did not have much soil; and they sprang up immediately, because they had no depth of soil. But after the sun rose, they were scorched, and because they had no root, they withered away. Others fell among the thorns, and the thorns came up and choked them out. But others fell on good soil and yielded a crop, some a hundred, some sixty, and some thirty times as much. The one who has ears, let him hear."*
>
> – Matthew 13:3-9

Now, it is interesting to note that Jesus does not start this parable with the words, "The kingdom of heaven is like..." as he does in so many of his other illustrations. This is because He is describing how the kingdom begins. It begins with the preaching of the Word, which then plants into the hearts of the people.

If this is true, and if it is true what the scripture proclaims when it says, "Faith comes by hearing, and hearing by the Word of God," then you and I need to be:

1. Reading the Bible daily.
2. On our knees in prayer to hear from the Lord

You cannot have faith without hearing so we can't miss that important first requirement. But when we hear, we need to have the right kind of soil so that the word grows into mature faith, which multiplies and spreads the goodness of God.

Let us break down the 4 soils that Christ mentions.

The Roadside

Jesus says that the first soil that seeds hit is the ground by the road. This would mean it is untilled, hard ground. You can imagine how compacted the dirt gets when it is traveled over constantly, every footfall and hoofbeat beating it down repeatedly. This kind of ground cannot even be dug into with a shovel – you need a pickaxe, or better yet a tractor! Or hardness wasn't what Jesus was going for, and it's just that this soil is so close to the comings and goings of everything under the sun, and it's so exposed to the air, that it's easy pickings for the birds. Either way, the lesson is clear: The dirt is not prepared for planting, so this seed is not hidden in the heart. It doesn't go down into the soil. It lies on top, where the devil can easily pluck it away, safely destroyed before it can take root and save anybody.

> *When anyone hears the word of the kingdom and does not understand it, the evil one comes and snatches away what has been sown in his heart. This is the one sown with seed beside the road.*
> – Matthew 13:19

Hearing God's Word is a precious gift! And it will be stolen away from us if we don't value it enough to keep it, to remember it, and to seek understanding. We cannot allow apathy and ignorance to steal our chance to enter the kingdom.

Rocky Soil

In Israel, there is a lot of limestone. And in some places, there will be ledges of rock that jut out with thin layers of soil on top of them. But it isn't very deep. Only a half-inch or inch down, impenetrable rock limits where roots can go. The soil may look ok on the surface, but it's only going to go so deep, and then it can't go any further.

We spoke in an earlier chapter about the sort of person who only wants enough faith to avoid Hell, but he doesn't really want more of God. He just wants to avoid a bad consequence. Unfortunately, I think that group makes up a portion of the "rocky soil" population. Their understanding is surface level, their commitment is dependent upon comfort, and when they get any pushback, their shallow roots are not enough to revive them afterwards.

They've got no backbone in faith, unfortunately.

> *The one sown with seed on the rocky places, this is the one who hears the word and immediately receives it with joy; yet he has no firm root in himself, but is only temporary, and when affliction or persecution occurs because of the word, immediately he falls away.*
> – Matthew 13:20

Wiersbe puts it this way:

> "In the parable, the sun represents persecution that comes because of the Word. Persecution helps believers grow. But the sunshine will kill a plant with no roots."

For all you gardeners out there, you know this to be true. A plant with shallow roots doesn't have it in them to resist the heat of the day. A plant with deep roots pulls up water from the ground, even in dry times, and so it can bounce back even after withering. It is connected to a good source of water and nutrients, and it is securely anchored.

The sun shines every day, you might have noticed, and there hasn't yet been alive a single man or woman who hasn't suffered. The key for the believer to endure that suffering without losing their faith, is to be deeply rooted in God's words.

Even when you are depleted, you can be refreshed. There is infrastructure in place to supply you with what you need to stay alive. There is a foundation to hold you up, or raise you back up, even when you fall over. But without a deep root, none of that can happen. Roots cannot go deep in a few days or a weekend, it takes time. Make a commitment today to grow your faith roots deeper. When we allow our growth to stop or be delayed, it impacts the Kingdom and others counting on us to be strong for them.

We used to study the Bible in schools in this country, so that all children had some kind of root in the scriptures. Now, sadly, this is the exception and not the rule. We've booted the Bible out of public schools, and unless a child attends a religious institution or attends A.W.A.N.A. (Kids Bible Program), or if their parents are very engaged and active in teaching them scripture, most people grow up without a deep root in our faith. This means that they will have to acquire it when they're older, at some point, when life is busier, there is more unlearning to do to make room for the learning, and, in general, it is more difficult. Pew research says 34% of Christians come to Christ between the ages of 5-14 years old, from 14-30 the percentage drops to 4%. We must reach the children with the love of Jesus.

I believe it can be done. If we are to have faith that lasts, grows, and produces good fruit, we need roots that go all the way down, not just a half-inch before hitting limestone. Let's remember Psalm 127:3 "Behold, children are a heritage from the Lord, the fruit of the womb a reward."

Thorny Soil

Some seed fell on the ground among the thorns. The thorns "grew up" or "sprang up," meaning the weed seeds were already in the ground. Then, these fast-growing space hoarders assume all of the room, and our tender young crops can't get any sunshine, water, or nutrients. This kind of soil crowds out the good seed of the Word.

Perhaps this soil would otherwise work well for the seeds, but there is just too much else going on.

Listen, the devil can steal away surface-level faith, persecution and troublesome times can wither faith that only has shallow roots, but *even plants with deeper roots and better soil can be defeated.*

Isn't that tragic?

A man or woman of sincere faith, who starts letting their financial troubles, career goals, lust for entertainment, obsession over relationships, or any number of other things, take up more and more of their attention may find one day that their potentially good faith has been choked out by everything else they deemed more important.

God will suffer no rivals (Nahum 1:2). He'll either be king of your heart or He won't be, but God's never the vice-president of a heart. He's never the duke, the attorney general, or second in command. He won't be your doddering grandfather. The Lord will be your Father, or He won't be.

As Jesus famously said,

> *You can't serve God and Mammon [the god of money].*
> – Matthew 6:24

Let's look at how Jesus describes the thorny soil:

> *And the one sown with seed among the thorns, this is the one who hears the word, and the anxiety of the world and the deceitfulness of wealth choke on the word, and it becomes unfruitful.*
> – Matthew 13:22

Did you catch that? Blink, and you miss it. Jesus' words are all so deliberately chosen and rich in meaning, that we have to read carefully. He says, "and it becomes unfruitful," meaning that there is still a plant there!

See, the devil doesn't have to kill you to win. He can just make you useless and ineffective. He can box you in. Even if you understand the word and receive it, if you aren't fighting the good fight, are you really in the kingdom? Or have the concerns of this world caged you in?

Jesus teaches elsewhere, like in the Sermon on the Mount, about trusting in God for our provision, and on not worrying but trusting God. But here, all we need to remember is this:

Faith puts God and His Word first. Everything else is seen through the lens of faith. Otherwise, what is the point? Who cares if your corn stalk grows if it doesn't produce any corn?

Good Soil

After hearing about three ways, we can miss it, finally we find a soil that the seed can thrive and grow in. This soil is prepared, has space for deep roots, and isn't infested with weeds. But even here, Jesus draws a distinction. He says that the seeds here bear fruit and produce a hundred, sixty, or thirty times as much as was planted.

Do you see it? Three kinds of bad soil, three kinds of good soil.

All of the seeds sown here on good soil yield saving faith. But not all of it yields the same amount of fruit. Not all believers are equally fruitful, even though all are fruitful to some extent.

The soil determines the outcome.

> *But the one sown with seed on the good soil, this is the one who hears the word and understands it, who indeed bears good fruit and produces, some a hundred, some sixty, and some thirty times as much.*
>
> – Matthew 13:23

We must also receive this word into our hearts to enter this blessed fourth soil. The Greek word for "receive" means to accept deliberately, willingly, favorably, and readily and to embrace with favor and delight. It is far more than an indifferent or apathetic reception but is a loving reception with great delight and love. You must be intentional in your faith journey.

We can never be careless with the soil of our heart, for the soil determines whether the Word of God will produce fruit. Our heart is God's field, and we are farmers together with God. We must cultivate the soil of our heart with Him so that it continually produces a harvest to His glory.

Don't miss this – a lot of times, we read the parable of the sower and read it like it's talking about everybody else.

Mary? Oh, she's thorny soil, choked out by the cares of this world. Jim? He's good soil. Maybe a sixty-fold kind of guy. Derek? He's roadside, for sure. No use preaching to him.

This, unfortunately, misses the main point:

This parable is about you. Try re-reading it asking what soil are you today? Are you having a growing faith season?

You are supposed to leave it asking yourself, "Which one of the four soils am I?"

Saint Paul has something to say about this:

> *Test yourselves to see if you are in the faith; examine yourselves! Or do you not recognize this about yourselves, that Jesus Christ is in you – unless indeed you fail the test? But I trust that you will realize that we ourselves do not fail the test. For we can do nothing against the truth, but only for the truth.*
> – 2 Corinthians 13:5-6, 8

We need to examine ourselves honestly, while this is top of mind, lest the devil snatch away the seed of faith, or the sun scorches it, or the weeds choke it out. But we have to keep in mind an admonition from Dr. Tony Evans:

> *"If God's Word is not working, you need to check the ground it landed on, because there is nothing wrong with the seed."*

Restoring the Ground

If you examine yourself and realize, "I don't really understand the Word," or, "I have a shallow commitment," and you come to find that your heart is not made up of good soil, I have good news for you – God can still do a work in you.

But He's asking you to partner with Him. That means you must be intentional in collaborating along with God's Word and Spirit in your life.

Gardeners don't always start with pristine soil. Thankfully, there is a way to restore subpar ground. First, if it's really bad – hard, compacted, nearly concrete stuff – then it needs to be broken up. The old ideas and attitudes in you may need to be shaken up. Whatever isn't yielding godly fruit needs to be examined, raked over, and plowed. Jeremiah the prophet once even said to Israel,

> *Break up your fallow [barren, unproductive, uncultivated] ground,*
> *and do not sow among thorns.*
>
> *– Jeremiah 4:3*

Then, when that's done, it's time to compost. This takes work on your part mentally, spiritually, and physically.

If you aren't into agriculture, that means the process of breaking good ingredients down into nutrition for the soil, to be laid over the top and mixed in, so that their minerals and vitamins can seep into the turned up, infertile soil and make it fertile ground.

This process takes some time, and it requires water, and regular stirring. This means we need to take the time to add prayer to our lives, searching out wisdom, reading the Bible, and letting it sink down into us, turning it into action, and mixing it into our previously unfruitful lives. With enough of this, the old ground becomes new ground, ready to receive seeds to grow and produce the fruit of the spirit.

Tony Evans, again, hits it out of the park:

> *Hearing the Bible preached is like eating an appetizer. Once you hear the sermon, no matter how much you liked it or enjoyed it, all you got was the appetizer. The full meal comes when you take the Word you have heard and process it, digest it, and put it to use in your daily life… There is nothing wrong with the seed because the seed is the Word of God and therefore the Word of God is perfect. The damage is in the soil.*

Even when we've made a mistake or find ourselves on the wrong path, and we wonder if God can forgive us, we can look to the illustration of the soils for encouragement. Decomposed plant parts and animal waste (Yes, animal waste) are prime components of good compost. God, who is ever resourceful, can use the broken things in our lives, the mistakes we've made, and even our flaws, to break down and turn into wisdom, experience, humility, and openness to the truth. Even the most dry, worthless soil can be restored and once again teem with life.

If you need to reestablish the soil of your heart, here are some good ingredients for godly compost:

1. Studying the Word of God, read with an intent to take notes and look up words you are not aware of their meaning.
2. Fasting, praying, righteous living, and seeking the mind of Christ... become sensitive to the Holy Spirit.
3. Learning your spiritual gifts and investing them in kingdom work. We all have at least one gift to give back.
4. Being a giver, more than a taker!
5. Following Jesus faithfully, becoming someone who reaches others for Christ, and taking your faith seriously.

Chapter 3

Moving Mountains by Faith

Since I am a sports fan, there are many times I have faced failure – but also victory. In any sort of competition, you must train, focus, and, at times, learn to have goals, strategy, and plans. Nevertheless, in the heat of the moment, things outside of your control can happen. Being a Tennessee football fan, I can tell you many occasions where we have been disappointed, after thinking, "This is the year." Then, after that heavy dose of hopeium fails, we have to accept that some things are not meant to be. That does not mean your plans or goals were a waste; sometimes they serve a purpose greater than you could have imagined.

Let me share the true story of Olympian Derek Redmond:

Derek Redmond of Great Britain had dreamed all his life of winning a gold medal in the 400-meter race, and his dream was in sight as the gun sounded in the semifinals at Barcelona. He was running the race of his life and could see the finish line as he rounded the turn into the backstretch. Suddenly, he felt a sharp pain go up the back of his leg. He fell face first onto the track with a torn right hamstring.

Sports Illustrated recorded the dramatic events:

> As the medical attendants were approaching, Redmond fought to his feet. "It was animal instinct," 'he would say later. He set out hopping, in a crazed attempt to finish the race. When he reached the stretch, a large man in a T-shirt came out of the stands, hurled aside a security guard, and ran to Redmond, embracing him. It was Jim

Redmond, Derek's father. "You don't have to do this," he told his weeping son. "Yes, I do," said Derek. "Well, then," said Jim, "we're going to finish this together." And they did.

Fighting off security men, the son's head sometimes buried in his father's shoulder, they stayed in Derek's lane all the way to the end, as the crowd gaped, then rose and howled and wept. Derek didn't walk away with the gold medal, but he walked away with an incredible memory of a father who, when he saw his son in pain, left his seat in the stands to help him finish the race.

Put yourself in Derek's shoes, just after his hamstring tore. The prospect of finishing the race seemed impossible. A mountain loomed before him, and he stared up at it like an ant.

But what did he do?

He fought to his feet. He leaned into the adrenaline, and he hopped. Fighting the pain, discomfort, and embarrassment. He waved off people wanting to take him out of the race.

At first, it seemed like he was going to make it. He was hopping like a man on a mission, determined to uphold his country's grand tradition of sportsmanship and honor by finishing the race.

Up in the stands there was some commotion. A man was pushing through security to come onto the field. As a dozen officers tried to stop him, this man pushed his way onto the track toward the wounded runner that by this point started to slow down. Then it was at that moment that the man that pushed through security appeared and hugged the runner; it was his son. The father then had his wounded son place his arm around him and his father helped him finish the race. The Olympic crowd erupted in applause as if he had won the gold medal. You see, people like to witness winners at all levels, just finish the race.

We read in II Timothy 4:7-8 "7 I have fought the good fight, I have finished the race, I have kept the faith. 8 Now there is in store for me the crown of righteousness, which the Lord, the righteous Judge, will award to me on that day—and not only to me, but also to all who have longed for his appearing."

This is what God does for us. When we are experiencing pain and we're struggling to finish the race, we can be confident that we have a loving Father who won't let us do it alone. He left His place in heaven to come alongside us in the person of His Son, Jesus Christ. "I am with you always," says Jesus, "to the very end of the age" (Matt. 28:20).

Mountains are big to us, and our efforts small in comparison, but God dwarfs them all. His size is the only size that matters. And if he puts His thumb on the scale, there isn't a single thing we can't accomplish.

"It is not the size of the mountain in your view but the size of the mountain within you that matters." (Macilism) You sometimes have to dig deep down inside of your heart of hearts to achieve the faith victory. Life is messy and tough but with God it can work!

We see this in the Word, in Matthew 17.

> *When they came to a crowd, a man came up to Jesus, falling on his knees before him, saying, "Lord, have mercy on my son, because he has seizures and suffers terribly; for he often falls into the fire and often into the water. And I brought him to your disciples, and they could not cure him." And Jesus answered and said, "You unbelieving and perverse generation, how long shall I put up with you? Bring him here to me." And Jesus rebuked him, and the demon came out of him, and the boy was healed at once.*
> – Matthew 17:14-18

We haven't gotten to the mountains part yet, but this first part of the story is worth looking at closely.

Jesus has just come off the Mount of Transfiguration, and as he returns to His disciples who were not with Him, He finds that they were not able to conduct His work in His absence. Jesus sounds harsh here as he says, "How long shall I put up with you?" but we need to read those words in context. Imagine a physician at a hospital, who comes into a room where his attending doctors have been treating a patient who is in a lot of pain – and they're doing it all wrong. His frustration is not out of pride; it is out of compassion for the one who is suffering. "Why didn't you help this man the way you should have?" you can picture him rightfully saying. I believe that's what Jesus is getting at here. He has compassion for those who are in trouble and suffering, and for those of us who have raised our hands to say, "We'll do your work, Lord," He wants us to do His work successfully.

But Jesus won't leave the boy in his agony. He takes it upon Himself to drive out the demon and restore the child to health.

The chapter continues:

> *Then the disciples came to Jesus privately and said, "Why could we not cast it out?" And He said to them, "Because of your meager faith; for truly I say to you, if you have faith the size of a mustard seed, you will say to this mountain, 'Move from here to there,' and it will move; and nothing will be impossible for you. But this kind does not go out except by prayer and fasting."*
>
> – Matthew 17:19-21

Oftentimes, when people read the Bible, they flip it open to a random page, jab their finger into the text, and say, "This is about my life" and to be fair, sometimes maybe it is. The Bible is a collection of 66 Holy-Spirit-inspired books, written by diverse writers to all kinds of different people. As a Youth Pastor I came up with the 3 A's to teach my students to follow when they were studying scripture:

- Author
- Audience
- Application

(Example of the 3 A's using LUKE: Go to the gospel of Luke and see the Author is Luke, an educated man that was doctor. The Audience is Most Excellent Theophilus. The Application is the life of Jesus Christ. Many do not realize ACTS is basically Luke 2. Look at author of ACTS; Luke, the Audience is just Theophilus (dropped the title because they have a relationship now), then the Applications is about the CHURCH! Notice in ACTS Paul shares his three missionary journeys but also his testimony three times.)

Who wrote the Gospel of Matthew? "Who was Matthew?" is helpful in our reading and studying. Matthew, one of Jesus' 12 disciples and an eyewitness of His ministry, was a Levite – a member of Israel's priestly class. And when Jesus called Him, he was in sin. He'd turned his back on his role in the kingdom of God and on his people, and he went to work for the Roman oppressors.

God has a way of redeeming our mistakes and bringing us to fulfill His purposes for us, doesn't He?

Matthew was an outsider, an outcast, but still one of God's people, called to be a priest. He understood failure, and forgiveness. He left the tribe of Levi, priest hood, to become a man of wealth as a tax collector for the enemy at the time, Romans.

What about #2 Audience? Who was the Gospel of Matthew written to? For some of us, this will sound like an odd question, or something we've never thought to ask before. Isn't the Bible for everyone?

The answer to that is, "Of course the Bible is for everyone to learn from." But each book still had an original audience. And the Gospel of Matthew was written to a Jewish audience, to convince them that Jesus is the Messiah, the visible Yahweh.

Now we look at #3, application, or what this means to us.

Jesus seemed to like mountains. He prayed on the mountains, went up for the Transfiguration, taught His most famous sermon on the Mount of Olives, and referenced them in His teaching. I think part of the reason is because we can identify with a mountain being so much bigger than us, something daunting looking down over us.

In Matthew 17, Jesus was physically standing next to a mountain when he told His disciples "You will say to this mountain" (emphasis added). It was a teaching aid.

So, don't climb Mt. Shasta, clench your fists, and try to throw it into the ocean with mystical willpower. People get weird with this passage sometimes. God isn't saying that you have the esoteric power of pure will to manifest whatever you want in front of you. He is saying, "Open the door to God working even just a little bit, and watch as He rushes in."

God can literally move a mountain, part the Red Sea, or do a host of miracles today, as the Bible tells us, but the bigger miracle is when we, in our faith, are moved to serve Him. In the book of Jonah, God moved a mountain in his life to overcome bigotry, disobedience, and anger. In many ways, the human heart is the final frontier, and God can do great things with even a little bit of faith.

A mustard seed is a tiny seed, folks. It doesn't take much. But remember that faith is not some isolated, formless thing. We have faith in something or someone so if you have even a small amount of faith in God and you begin to do His work, He'll put His thumb on the scales.

People use this passage in Matthew to promote a "Name It and Claim It" gospel, unfortunately. They'll teach that this means, "Imagine that big fancy house on the beach. Claim it! Manifest it! Have just a little faith and do your affirmations, and God's gonna give you that house!"

When a preacher talks about your personal finances as the lead topic in a church you might be cautious. Money, wealth, items of value are not bad in themselves. What makes wealth a battle of faith is we tend to lean on what man can provide over believing in God and his supernatural provisions. Moving a mountain just for show is not God's style, he moves things for His glory not ours.

On many occasions, Jesus' followers *left* wealthy lifestyles to follow him. Matthew and Zacchaeus were tax collectors. Peter, Andrew, James, and John were fishermen. When you study carefully, you'll see the people that walked close to Jesus were not becoming wealthy but becoming dependent on God to provide. The one exception was Judas, with the most expensive kiss in human history for 30 pieces of silver.[5] The other thing we are told about Judas is that he was the treasurer, so he had the trust of his peers. Yet at the Last Supper, the Bible tells us "Satan entered him." I'm of the opinion that this was most likely a slow fade, starting with questioning why certain amounts should be spent on Jesus, like he did when Mary anointed Jesus' feet with expensive perfume. Judas tried to rebuke her, and Jesus then rebuked him... Is it possible the devil made Judas think Jesus was living lavishly, and therefore so, should he? Was a seed of jealousy planted in his heart?

Be wise and not let your faith be tainted by materialism as your only means of measuring success and approval. Your spiritual bank should be more important than an earthly one. A spiritual bank keeps accounts of things that will matter in heaven once you have left earth.

The real meaning of this passage about moving mountains is that it is so wonderful and so helpful in our daily lives and our journey of faith.

The Letter of James in the New Testament talks about this same issue:

You do not have because you do not ask.

– James 4:2b

But don't stop there! Keep reading.

> *You ask and do not receive, because you ask with wrong motives, so that you may spend what you request on your pleasures… "God is opposed to the proud but gives grace to the humble." Submit therefore to God.*
>
> – James 4:3, 6b-7

God never promises to give us absolutely whatever we want if we just believe it hard enough. He promises to show up if we are in league with Him, going where He is going, doing the work that He is doing.

He won't leave His own out to dry if we trust Him, have faith, and get up and start the process of finishing the race.

1 John makes this a little clearer.

> *Beloved, if our heart does not condemn us, we have confidence before God; and whatever we ask, we receive from Him, because we keep His commandments and do the things that are pleasing in His sight. This is His commandment, that we believe in the name of His Son Jesus Christ, and love one another, just as He commanded us.*
>
> 1 John 3:21-23

Just in case we missed it, later in his letter, the apostle John says it again.

> *This is the confidence which we have before Him, that, if we ask anything according to His will, He hears us. And if we know that He hears us in whatever we ask, we know that we have the requests which we have asked from Him.*
>
> – 1 John 5:14-15

He won't leave us hanging.

The disciples were asked to cast out a demon and heal a suffering boy. They didn't have faith that God would make up the gap between what they could accomplish and what needed to be done. That's why Jesus called them "faithless" in his frustration.

After Jesus' death, burial, and resurrection, they finally learned that the Messiah was different than they had imagined, and they had laid aside their jockeying for position, and had fully embraced the call to God's work. The disciples spread Christianity throughout the known world, healed the sick, cast out demons, fed the hungry and changed the world.

They moved many mountains.

The key is, they were in fellowship with God. They learned His compassion, His desire to take care of the stranger, the orphan, and the widow. They asked Him to move mountains that God wanted to move, and He responded in power.

Do you suffer with any kind of addiction that affects your relationships, drains your bank account, and keeps you from doing God's work? Ask him to move those mountains and believe that He will! But if you believe that He's going to move that mountain, you'll then go and take the first step, won't you?

Pour that whiskey down the drain, and expect God to meet you in your need, and give you the strength to overcome.

Many addictions such as porn, gambling, drugs and even social media can take your time, attention and passions to the dark side of sin. Your time is valuable and how you use it, invest it or waist it matters to the God who is the giver of all things.

Is there a person you have on your heart who needs to hear God's message of forgiveness and salvation, but you are afraid? Ask God to move that mountain of fear in your heart, and then act. He will be with you.

In Matthew 9, Jesus is touched by the great needs of the people he sees.

> *Seeing the crowds, He felt compassion for them, because they were distressed and downcast, like sheep without a shepherd. Then He said to His disciples, "The harvest is plentiful, but the workers are few. Therefore, plead with the Lord of the harvest to send out workers into His harvest."*
>
> *– Matthew 9:36-38*

Do you see His compassion? That's what He was trying to teach His disciples to see the world with kingdom eyes. Align your heart with the heart of God, and when you do that, you will want to help heal the world, spread God's good news, and make what is bent and crooked, straight.

Believe that He will aid you in that work.

He will come alongside you to get rid of sin in your life, to provide for the needy, to provide for you to do the work that He has called you to.

"But this kind comes out only by prayer and fasting," Jesus says. We need to do the preparation of walking closely with God. How else can we be close enough with Him to have the same desires that He has?

We have to pray in the spirit to connect to God. I like to say, "Stay strong, pray long." Selfish prayers tend to be short and short-sighted. It isn't the number of words or the number of minutes that makes a good prayer, but it is a pressing into the heart of God. Spend time with Him if you want to know Him. Then you will be able to move the mountains that He wants to move.

Most people tend to pray for their own needs, and as far as it goes, there isn't anything wrong with those prayers, but we don't want to miss out on all of the aspects of prayer, spending time in His presence. Over the years, there have been a number of helpful acrostics people have developed to help us pray. You may have heard of "A.S.K." which stands for: Ask, Seek, and Knock

Or others use the formula "A.C.T.S." which means:

- Adoration (tell God what you love about Him)
- Confession
- Thanksgiving
- Supplication (asking for things)

However, you go about your prayer life, remember that the point is to get closer to God. This requires humility, patience, openness, and time. But God will meet us in our lack if we have faith in Him and take the first step of trying.

Yes, God even helps us pray, if we have faith and give it an honest try and keep trying.

Then, our prayers begin to change as we spend time with the Lord. And we can then pray with real power and effect.

If you spend all of your time with money and all of your thoughts on how to make more money, your prayers will tend to be about money.

Our minds are a wonderful gift from God to store information, as well as to adapt to what we engage with in our lives. Be a daily prayer person, who prays for His will over our own wills.

Here's another "Macilism" for you: "If you lay with dogs, you're gonna get fleas; if you hang with monkeys, you will swing from trees. Repent of sin and be set free."

If you spend time with God, He can shape your desires and your heart. Then you can really partner with Him.

Who do you think of when you imagine greatness?

If we want to be great, we're going to have to prepare and be motivated to follow the plans of faith.

The great Israelite King David, when he was a shepherd boy, killed lions and bears with his sling in private, as he protected his flock. Then, when Goliath came forth to disgrace the God of Israel and countrymen, David performed in public by killing the giant.

The story says that he gathered five smooth stones before taking on that giant. I don't think this was because he was afraid of missing; Goliath had four brothers, and David was prepared.

What do you practice in private? Be wise about it, for that is how you will perform in public, be it good or bad.

A great walk with God doesn't happen without preparation, which amounts to spending time with Him.

Then we can be prepared, even for the demons that don't come out except with prayer and fasting, and no mountain can hold us up for long.

And we all face mountains, don't we? They seem big from a distance, but when we're right up against them, they're downright gigantic. There are all kinds of mountains we'll need to move on our journey of faith, but in this book, we're going to focus on three big ones that everyone will have to contend with at some point in their lives, and we'll see how faith can remove and overcome.

We will look at the mountains of bitterness, division, and fear, and learn together how the Lord can lead us to forgiveness and joy, unity and community, and bold faith that pierces the darkness.

Pray for the Lord to teach you in this process, to help you apply the truth of His word and spend time with Him, so that you can understand His will for your life.

And if you have a minute, watch the original recording of Derek Redmond running that race in the 1992 Olympics on YouTube. Remember that God is like his father, He will be there for us to lien on when we cannot stand.

Section I: Summary

The Journey of Faith

- In order to live out the journey of faith, we need to know what (and Who) we are putting our faith in.

- Faith is trusting in God, and that will result in being willing to step out boldly where God is directing you, even if you don't have all of the answers yet.

- Faith is doing things God's way, even when that looks strange to the rest of the world.

- We each need to examine our hearts to figure out what kind of soil we have. Are we like the roadside? Rocky soil? Thorny soil? Or good soil?

- Make a habit of "spiritual composting." Add things into your life and daily habits that will help to change the soil of your heart, to make it more receptive to the Holy Spirit's good work in you.

- Faith can move the mountains that God wants to move. Align your vision and goals with God's vision and goals.

SECTION II:

Moving the Mountain of Bitterness

Chapter 4

The Overcoming Power of Forgiveness

I was blessed from the beginning with a good example of what the life of faith looks like. Let me tell you a little bit about my father, and you'll see what I mean:

My father has been a retired FBI Special Agent for nearly 30 years now. He, along with some other young men from the South, were recruited in part for their manners and values. My parents (high school sweethearts) got married and went to DC to work for the Bureau as my father went to night school to get his degree in accounting. They were always focused and hardworking, never complaining about the workload. By the time I came along, my father was stationed in Michigan, and shortly after that we moved to New Jersey. My first eight years I was raised a Yankee, and I loved it. Slurpee's, Frozen Mug Root beer stands, and my dirty bike pals rode until dark.

But even amid a demanding job and family life, my father made time to serve the Lord. Church planting in the 70's was not what it is today with the SBC. He was a worship leader throughout the years, and he and my mother helped to plant a church in New Jersey that later became Raritan Valley Baptist Church. This was where I got some of my first, lasting impressions of what it meant to step inside the church and let the Lord lead you down the path of faith. I remember one night at a revival meeting, I noticed people coming forward to respond to the service, in tears, and then they'd go back into a room to talk with somebody, and they'd come out smiling from ear to ear. So, I called it "The Happy Room," and I wondered what went on in there to take these upset people and make them glad.

The next night, I went into the happy room to check it out, and I found some kind people who explained what they were doing. It was a counseling room, where they explained to people what it meant to become a Christian, and how to live the life of faith.

My pastor, wisely noting my curiosity, set up a children's class for me and several others my age. After a few weeks of being taught the Bible, the meaning of salvation, and the purpose of baptism, the Lord's Supper... I concluded. I wanted what my father, mother and sister had. I wanted to live for Jesus, too.

I knelt down in my living room, with my daddy on one side and Pastor Heiglig on the other, with mom tearing up on the couch. She gave me a big hug once I asked Jesus to save me.

But then, a few months later, my life changed when dad was transferred to Mayberry. I'm only kidding – it was Tennessee, and I had cousins that talked funny and had bad grammar, but my parents explained that Johnson City was actually their hometown. We visited there every Christmas and at times in the summer, and we moved back to our roots, near all of the uncles, aunts, grandparents, and the like. Chattanooga is where we moved to, only three hours from the Tri-Cities my parents call home. After 18 years of living in Chattanooga, this is what I consider my hometown.

Once we moved to Chattanooga, we joined a church, and my father and mother were asked to be the youth ministers. We joined on my ninth birthday, and that church experience impacted my faith, because it was here that I was called to the ministry.

Our youth group was called "The One-Way Mission Team," and we would perform an hour-long program of singing and scripture, wearing matching outfits. Some would call it a "youth choir." My sister played the piano, and dad played the guitar.

For six years, The One-Way Mission Team made the trek from Chattanooga to Pennsylvania to help run a VBS, do backyard bible clubs, minor construction projects and sing in malls, churches, and nursing homes to tell people about Jesus.

Chattanooga has been called the "buckle of the Bible belt." That doesn't mean the place is perfect, but it does mean everybody, and their mother is in church on Sunday, or at least it was that way forty years ago. At minimum, everyone knew about Jesus and the stories in the Bible.

We introduced kids to Little Debbie snack cakes. It was there I first noticed hungry children that had no lunch or meals like we did. Some kids were locked out of their homes till their parents got off work and had no meal till dinner. This saddened my heart.

So, imagine my surprise when kids in Pennsylvania had conversations like this with me:

"Is Jesus one of the Super Friends?"

"One of what?" I asked.

"Like on a team with Superman and the Flash. He walks on water, things like that, right. Comic book stuff."

You might be tempted to think that this kid was pulling my leg, but he was entirely sincere. I mean, hey, Jesus is my superhero too, I guess, but Marvel didn't make Him up.

So that was a weird interaction, but the strangeness of it sorts of made it funny. Then I met another kid, and at 13 years old my heart broke.

He asked me why "Damn" was God's last name.

I tried to correct his mistake – but I was shaken up. I couldn't believe that someone in the United States of America was so unfamiliar with Christianity, that he thought God's last name was actually "Damn," as in when people curse.

Mind you, this was some decades ago, and kids didn't know who Jesus was. God started pulling on my heart.

I went back to my dorm room at Penn State and wept. I was reading the Bible and praying, and I had a moment with the Lord. Isaiah 6:8 "Then I heard the voice of the Lord saying, "Whom shall I send? And who will go for us?" And I said, "Here am I. Send me!" just jumped off the page and it was a soul changing moment. I surrendered to ministry that day, shared it with my parents and could just feel the Holy Spirit moving closer in my life.

The next Sunday, I went forward to the altar and did some business with God. I knelt down and told Him that I was surrendering to preach publicly what God had called me too privately. I then told my pastor and he shared with the church to pray with me and for me.

I'm here to say, don't be surprised if you offer to serve God, and He takes you up on it quickly. Because that, at least, is what happened to me. God started giving me speaking opportunities immediately, even as a teenager. Teaching an adults bible study class once as the teacher helped me prepare, youth events, banquets .... Relying on the spirit, I preached the Word.

I went into middle school full-bore, trying to evangelize all of my friends. I was on fire. One thing I had to learn was not to judge others. A good friend of mine at the time Terry Topping went to another denomination. His mother asked me over for a talk and explained they were another denomination, and that Baptist were not the only show in town. It was a great conversation and she then prayed for me; Mrs. Topping was a kind soul. Then my Catholic buddy Robby prayed to receive Christ and I bought him a study bible. It was then I realized about the extra books they had. Later in college Robbie was dating a committed Christian girl and he actually went to a revival service without her, and he had that bible I had given him, and he renewed his faith in Christ.

Sadly, in High School things were challenging to my faith. Many of my friends got tired of my message, praying over meals and inviting them to church events. They made an agreement with each other that went like this:

"Until Macil gets laid or gets drunk, we're not going to talk to him."

They took an actual vow of silence against me. Now, when your close friends with a group of kids show up one day to find that none of them will acknowledge you or speak to you, not even to explain why, is troubling. This is when High School started in the 10th grade, so something happened over the summer for many of them that separated our values. Plus, we had a middle school on Singal Mountain that merged with ours to form Red Bank High School. I found out later a kid named John from the mountain wanted in our gang and saw a way to unite them was to take my place.

I played basketball and football with these guys. They wouldn't even speak to me in the locker room. When I walked in the locker room they would literally turn and not talk to me.

So, distressed, I tried to get into a rhythm at school, but when I walked into my home room one day, there was a white t-shirt on my desk with the words "Macil is a queer" for everyone to see.

They had assumed that since I wasn't having sex like them (at age 14) and getting drunk, that I was a homosexual. So, they stopped speaking to me and instead tormented me in various ways. No longer invited to parties, spend the night, or hang out.

I remember the first time I went to the lunchroom after all this started. I had my food, I had forty-five minutes to eat, but I had no one to sit with. My friends had all turned on me, and they wouldn't let me sit with them at lunch.

I felt alone and for those of you reading who've ever been hurt, pushed around, traumatized, or harmed by someone who should have supported you, you know what I'm talking about. Sure, there is sadness or depression, but the other side of that coin is anger. When anger, if you sit on it long enough, turns into something else. This battle to fight bitterness was a good life lesson for me.

Another Macilism "Stay strong, pray long." Sometimes you have to get on your knees and weep. God knows before you ask but like any parent, they want to know you want their help.

This is where I had a choice to make, and where each of you has a choice to make as well. I could have hated my former friends. I could have gotten them back, somehow.

Not that I was a perfect teenager, my faults were many. All I knew was that I loved the Lord. My Catholic buddy Robbie came to me and said he would say he saw me get drunk and let's make up some names of girls saying I slept with them and then I am back in the gang. I said, "Robby if you are asking me to pick Jesus or you and the guys, I pick Jesus!" He said, don't ever try and talk to him again in public and he meant it. LOL the song has you heard about the lonesome loser... that was me at the time.

So, I was angry, felt betrayed and part of me wanted to be bitter but I chose better. I quit the basketball team and went to play church league to avoid the locker room antics. Then I wrote all their names down in my prayer journal and each night I would pray for them by name sincerely.

In the moment, moving on and seeking the good of those who hurt you usually does not seem appealing. And the world has an entirely different way.

Have you ever seen a "revenge film"? Movies like The Count of Monte Cristo, The Punisher, Django, or Unforgiven? It's a whole genre in Hollywood. Someone gets done wrong in a horrible way, and we root for the main character who bides his time, planning sweet revenge – usually violent, but sometimes just to ruin their enemy's entire life – and then we are gratified when they finally get to strike back!

This is the world's way. This is the mountain of bitterness. And, when we are mourning, lost, or hurting, it's appealing to let this obstacle stop us dead in our tracks, to submit to it. It's much easier to curl up at the foot of that mountain and go to sleep, rather than to move it out of our way. Moving a mountain always seems impossible.

The journey of faith doesn't have any shortcuts, however. There's no road around this mountain. If we want to follow Jesus, the only path is through, and that route is called forgiveness.

Jesus did not mince words when it comes to this topic:

> *"If you do not forgive other people, then your Father will not forgive your offenses."*
>
> – Matthew 6:15

That verse ought to scare us. I've heard far too many Christians either overlook this saying of Jesus' or try to convince themselves that it doesn't actually mean what it's saying, but there's not much to the interpretation on this one. If you don't forgive the people who wrong you, God won't forgive you.

And you need God to forgive you, right? I know I do.

It's God's way of saying, "Forgiveness is mandatory, Christian." God loved us while we were still sinners. He sent Jesus to teach us and then die an innocent man while we were His enemies. Jesus teaches in the Parable of the Unforgiving Servant in Matthew 18 the same thing!

I could go on, but the point is we all have a choice to make, like I had to make back when I was in high school:

Will you follow the parts of God's call that appeal to you? Or will you go all the way? Will you have faith that God's way is best, lean into Him, and forgive?

I knew I had to forgive, and so I did, to the best of my ability, and I prayed for my former friends, even when I had nobody to sit with in the lunchroom.

As it turned out, however, that loneliness didn't last too long. Two boys my age sat by themselves too, so I went over and joined them at their table. Apparently, they were the first two black students to attend Red Bank High School.

SECTION II: *Moving the Mountain of Bitterness*

Unfortunately, at the time this made them outcasts, but since I was an outcast too, we thought this was an okay basis to begin a friendship.

As time went on, I found out these two guys were kind, funny, honest, and interesting. And crucially, they didn't mind when I'd start lunch with a prayer. We made the most of our social status and had a good time in the cafeteria. I remember one day when one of the other boys asked, Macil, can I say the prayer today?

By the end of that year, more and more kids started joining our table, and suddenly it didn't seem so lonely, even though it still hurt getting kicked at and not being spoken to during football and basketball. Other kids felt like they didn't fit in either, so they found their way to us. It was like the island of misfit toys, and that was alright with us. My old friends still hadn't come around, but God gave me new friends. Then I realized what real friendship was, not just spending time but being concerned with a heart to help that person you call friend in time of need. I then realized many of the guys I hung around with were not really friends but just teammates that we had some fun times with. We all outgrow the playground of life and the games... as you become an adult you must learn discernment in your faith.

My Sophomore Year I got involved with Campus Crusade for Christ and Chuck Wallace took me in and mentored me. He saw the hazing and unkindness and would meet with me before school for prayer and discipleship. I went through six booklets in three years with Chuck. Part of that work was another opportunity to speak about God. There was an off-campus Bible study through Campus Crusade for Christ that met in the (huge) basement of a local doctor's house. They meet once a week on Thursday nights for a large group of kids from all over the area's schools. Chuck asked me to speak a few times in my sophomore year. Then My Junior and Senior year more often. It was like I was helping lead a small church of peers from all over Chattanooga.

By my senior year in high school, our lunch table grew to three table-lengths. If you can imagine every kid who ever felt rejected finding a place to feel welcomed, that was our spot in the cafeteria. I got attention for my play on the football team, I was the president of several clubs, and I was voted Mr. Redbank High School, FCA Christian Athlete of Redbank, and a number of other accolades that I had no idea God would give me. My peers had watched how I managed the hazing for believe me it was no secret. The unkindness, the untruths ... but you just love them in spite of it.

The reason I mention it is just that standing alone in the lunchroom at age 14, my first year of high school, it looked like the price of following Jesus was torment, loneliness, and social rejection. And, in fact, that was the cost. But I didn't realize at the time that there were also rewards for following Jesus. I gained a new community, even while I was rejected by the old community. In hindsight, I was far more blessed than put upon. Following Jesus does have a price, but it is always more than worth it.

If I hadn't forgiven my friends, I don't know if God would have given me the leadership and preaching opportunities that I had in high school. It's hard to share the love of Christ when you are filled with resentment for anyone. By the grace of God, this was a victory in my life, and I learned through experience that God's way is actually the best way. Amazingly, that wasn't all. God had more.

I remember when a girl named Becky came up to me in the lunchroom my senior year. She asked if we could step outside, and I said, "Sure."

She said, "Macil, I've watched how your friends turned on you these past two years. I want what you've got. Can you tell me how to be a Christian?"

I got to lead her to Christ, then. It was like God was telling me, "Macil, two years of this persecution was for a reason." It was to toughen me up, and to provide an example to some of my peers.

After that, one by one, my old friends started calling me. One guy told me over the phone, "Macil, I've got a gun to my head. Can you tell me one good reason I shouldn't pull the trigger?"

Another called me and said, "Macil, I think she's pregnant. What am I gonna do?"

Another one called me and said, "Macil, I'm depressed all the time. All these drugs and drinking just aren't doing it for me anymore, and that scares me."

See, I had told God at age 13 that I was surrendering to the call of ministry, and He accepted my offer. But God sets apart those who He uses. My friends saw that I was different, and when they were in crisis, they knew that I had something to offer them that wasn't the world's way, the failed solutions they'd been trying for so long.

I wasn't smarmy with them, and I never said, "I told you so." The thought of doing something like that never crossed my mind. God, in His goodness, was letting me be a minister to my old friends, so that they could have comfort, some

SECTION II: *Moving the Mountain of Bitterness*

sound advice, and a nudge back onto the path.

My friend Doug Hinshaw, who was one of the ringleaders in my group of tormentors back in the day. He got himself into a series of mishaps. He partied a lot, and subsequently he'd skip school. Because of that, he got benched, and despite being one of our best baseball players, he eventually got kicked off the team. Since he couldn't play baseball anymore, he quit school and didn't graduate with us.

He came to see me after graduation, and he was upset. He was angry at God, angry at the world. As we were sitting there, talking, I excused myself for a minute to go and get something, and when I came back, I found him crying. He found my journal while I was out of the room, and he read some of it. He said, "Macil, you were praying for us?"

I'd listed all of my old friends in that journal who made fun of me and made life difficult for me, and I prayed for each of them because Christ tells us to love our enemies – and I did.

In that moment, I got to tell him, "Yes, Doug. I prayed for you guys every day."

His crying turned to weeping then, and he asked for my forgiveness, which was easy for me, since I had already given it.

Doug, today, is one of my closest friends, and he's a pastor to boot. We have agreed whoever dies first the other will have his funeral. The Bible says,

> *Be angry, and yet do not sin; do not let the sun go down on your anger.*
>
> *– Ephesians 4:26*

This tells me that there are moments when you have to get past my hurt and anger. You must love people, even when they are un-loveable. .

In the next chapter, we'll talk more about this principle we find in Ephesians 4, and we'll look at how this helps us get through offenses with forgiveness instead of being overshadowed by the mountain of bitterness.

CHAPTER 5

The 12-Hour Anger Limit

Having an older sister, Michele, who would tease me like no other, anger was an early emotion I learned. She would practice the piano singing softly "Macil is a dummy dog." I went into anger mode and mom would come in asking what was wrong and she would say, "Mom I am practicing my piano lessons." One day mom came closer for Michele made this an almost daily ritual, and she realized my sister was pushing my buttons. Mom came to calm me down. We were later driving on an errand and Michele started her song and I erupted again, and mom said just call her a name. I said I can't think of one, them Mom said call her "Ralph." Michele then got upset and said, no fair mom you can't help him, and I then replied, "Shut up Ralph." If you have a sibling, you have moments like these of anger that will require forgiveness if families are to stay united.

I heard a true story one time of a British playwright named Frederick Lonsdale, who'd had a falling out with a fellow member of London's Garrick Club. One New Year's Eve, during the club's celebration, Seymour Hicks told Lonsdale that he really needed to reconcile with the guy. Lonsdale didn't want to. Hicks told him, "You must make peace with him, Frederick. It is very unkind to be unfriendly this time of year. Go over now and wish him a happy new year."

So, Lonsdale got up, crossed the room, and spoke to his enemy.

"I wish you a happy new year," he said, "but only one."

This is a man, who did not follow the Bible's instruction about having a 12-hour limit to his anger.

Let's drill down into that.

The apostle Paul, the man that the Holy Spirit used to write most of the New Testament, says this:

> *Be angry, and yet do not sin; do not let the sun go down on your anger, and do not give the devil an opportunity.*
>
> – Ephesians 4:26-27

Say what you will, but the Bible is an extremely practical book. I happen to think that's another way we know it's authentic and something we can trust. The Bible does not offer us a fantasy scenario where we never get angry, or where we never have a reason to get upset with somebody. It recognizes that life is messy, and we're living with all of these broken people – and we're sort of broken too. Stuff is going to go down from time to time. People are going to be unkind to you sometimes. People are going to be unfair to you. But you've got to remember the 12-hour anger limit.

The Bible says you can get angry. It says, "Yeah, that's cool, but you're not to let the sun go down on your anger."

And why is that? What is the big deal about keeping anger when someone has hurt you, if it's ok to get mad in the first place?

Bitterness is like drinking poison and hoping the other person dies, as they say, and boy is that the truth. And the thing about bitterness is that it takes up your whole view when you're in the thick of it. You can't see what else lies ahead when you're bitter. You can't see the sky. You can't count your blessings. The mountain of bitterness blocks you from continuing the journey of faith, and come hell or high water, it's a mountain that faith needs to move.

I'll quote another song, by a Christian artist named Lecrae:

> *"They say don't get bitter, get better,*
>
> *I'm working on switching those letters…"*

I like to ask people the question, "How many times a day should a Christian say the F-word?" Now, a lot of people will say zero, but I say, "Say it daily! Often! Say the F-word multiple times a day if you have to." …Of course, the F-word I'm referring to is "forgive," and if you've had a little laugh at my wordplay, you're welcome to it, but the point remains. We treat saying "I forgive you" like it's more offensive than saying a cuss word in public. We struggle with saying, and meaning, "I forgive you" when someone has done wrong. We worry that they'll take forgiveness as a license to do more bad behavior, or that they'll think they haven't really hurt us when they actually have. But we are called to forgive, as Christians.

I've had to battle with this. I think we all have, because a lot of people out their deal with feeling betrayed or cut out of a family or friend group. Experiencing anger is part of the process of dealing with difficult or unjust circumstances. But we can't stop there. Be angry, but don't sin. Then, make sure you forgive before the sun goes down, thus the 12-hour anger rule!

Understand, forgiving doesn't mean you're saying what someone did was the right thing to do. It means that you trust God to oversee it. He is just, even as He is merciful and compassionate. He gives people chances to turn from their sin, but eventually, He will sort it all out. David broke all ten commandments and yet when he died, he was known as a man after God's own heart for he sought and gave out forgiveness.

There have been several times in my life that I have felt betrayed, misquoted, misunderstood, and a victim of unkindness. As a youth pastor and pastor there were times I was persecuted for befriending people of color. There was literally a church in Mississippi, where I was youth pastor, which sent a young black teenager back to his seat but welcomed a young white teen into membership. As I drove the young man home, I asked why he didn't join. I didn't know what had happened, so he explained that he tried to join but was told to go back and think about what he was doing.

He then said, "Bro Macil, I have asked Jesus to save me, and I want to be baptized and join the church."

I said, "Come down the left side like the young lady did tonight and talk to me." (As youth pastor, I stood on the left side.) He did like I suggested, and I filled out his membership card and gave it to the pastor. We voted him in, but I was later chastised for it. He was the first black member of this First Baptist Church was evidently a major adjustment for a church in Mississippi in the 90's.

We had a basketball bible study in the gym as part of a seminary project for reaching the community. You came to a thirty-minute bible study and then played an hour and a half round robin tournament. The catch was, you could not play if you skipped the bible study. We had over a hundred and twenty people participate. As it happened, over 60% were young men of color. Because of that, the deacons called me in, shut the gym down for three months, and told me not to do this again.

The young man that had joined the church endured a lot of un-kindnesses, passing the offering plate past him to imply he had nothing to give. I usually paid for his Wednesday night meal, and one deacon told me to make him work and not give him a free ride. God saw it all, and this young man kept coming. He entered the Christian speech competition and won the local, regional, and eventually the Mississippi state speech tournament, a process which took about four months. His topic was "The Concentric Circles of Evangelism," and he talked about how we all meet a person daily with whom we can share the love of Christ. One by one, bigots got their hearts right. Several of the men that had been unkind later apologized to this young man. He went on to Vanderbilt on a full academic scholarship. He loved the unkind and hateful when they were at their worst. Pastor PJ Scott and I were at a Baptist assembly and one of the Pastors asked from the floor to Dr. Scott "Tell us about that colored boy that joined your church PJ." Pastor Scott, my diet coke pal, didn't miss the opportunity to share that this young man has changed our church. P.J went on to say even me, and with tears he told the other pastors at that meeting that this young man has moved the mountain of bigotry out of our church! That was a Move My Mountain moment I will never forget.

At another church I worked at in Charlotte, North Carolina, a young black man proposed to a young white lady at the end of a church service. Four families got up and left and later told me they would not be back because they do not believe in race mixing. When I performed their wedding, they asked me to share the gospel, and ten people came forward. May Chairman of Deacons told me at the wedding he was thinking of leaving the church over me performing this ceremony. I said, you just helped me lead people to Christ that came forward, how can you have these feelings. He just told me he could not support mixed marriages and was not happy with the young black men in our youth group and this might become a trend. He came at me later for allowing a black pastor friend of mine to preach a revival, and for baptizing black football players I had led to Christ.

Praying for bigots in a church is hard at times for if they are in leadership, they use their titles for secret meetings of disunity. God is bigger than the mountain of bigotry and I saw God move in once and was praying He could do it again in Charlotte.

SECTION II: *Moving the Mountain of Bitterness*

This church had several actions of unkindness and evil. We did 24-hour prayer services, fasts, and intercession with the good folks, but sadly this church was just unkind. Every pastor they had before us was treated badly, and there was a crowd determined to give me the same treatment. Every lie known to man was told or implied about the preachers before me, and then to me as well.

This was a whole new level of spiritual warfare. This was the first time that I felt, in my spirit, that we were never going to overcome in that place. Sadly, we left that church after eight years of battling, with many scars and painful memories. Watching my wife and children experience mistreatment was the worst part. I would lay on my face at night outside my daughters' rooms as they slept, begging God to spare them of the evil we were facing.

How do you forgive people who lie, who rally people against you to lie, and who even hold secret meetings in their homes to plan your demise? I felt like Jeremiah the weeping prophet, crying for the sheep that were being attacked in vicious ways.

In the middle of the pain, we were able to see several teenagers launched into ministry, we went door to door and canvased 52 neighborhoods with the gospel of Jesus, led the association in baptisms for many years, and we were able to send mission teams into Charlotte, other parts of North Carolina, New York, and Ecuador. I was also asked to speak at the Billy Graham Evangelistic Association nine times for their chapel services.

Another Macilism; "When there is great opportunity in front of you, expect great opposition from Satan."

The stories I could tell you might make you wonder if these people even knew Christ. Never in my life have I felt spiritual oppression like at that church. My personal secretary and others did 40 day fasts and begged God to overcome the evil, but this was the one-time God chose not to conquer as I thought he might. Years went by and one by one many of those evil-minded people had misfortune that appeared to be the hand of God. But I forgave them all. It took longer for some but through God's grace not only did I forgive them, but it made me stronger in my prayer life.

Five deacons from that Charlotte church asked me to forgive them. One was deeply involved and hosted one of the private meetings. I will be honest I first told him no, I can't forgive you hosting meetings of lies and not at least allow me to be present. I then could not sleep; I called him the next day and not only forgave him but asked that he forgive my hard heart. You see I thought I had forgiven them until they called or came to me. We are human failed vessels and Jesus reminded me that forgiveness is not agreement with their actions but a release of the baggage it has on your heart.

Forgiveness is a process at times, in that people can be unkind and vindictive over and over, and you feel yourself asking, "How can I forgive them when they kept being so hateful?" Welcome to the world of Jesus. He was constantly misquoted, misrepresented, and every time he loved certain communities, there were some that just returned hatred.

Hoping for the good of those who do wrong does not mean that you wish for them to blithely profit off of evil. It doesn't mean you hope they steal, kill, and manipulate, then go to bed with a smile on their faces and big deposits in their bank accounts. It means that you hope for their actual good – for repentance from sin, that they would have a clean conscience, God's spirit in their lives, and that they would feel the joy that comes from living a good life, God's way.

I needed to hope not for their destruction, but for their redemption. If even Jesus could say, "Father, forgive them," as evil men crucified Him, then we can say, "Father, I pray for their good and Your glory," and mean it.

Then the burden is off of our hearts. The question of justice is in God's hands.

God is full of compassion, mercy, love, and patience. But I tell you what, I'd be afraid to do evil in his name. I'd be terrified to keep someone out of his kingdom because of their skin color. Seems to me that God takes that sort of thing personally.

God is better than us, and He is right to give people time and patience.

In any case, the 12-hour anger limit is there for our protection. It's for our own good. In the Bible, we meet a character who violated this rule, and it was his downfall.

It's safe to say that King David was not the best father. His children had all sorts of misadventures, but the most tragic father-son debacle happened with his son Absalom. Absalom launched a revolt against David, his dad, and ran him out of the capital city. Absalom seemed well on his way to victory, and so he asked Ahithophel, one of David's close advisors who stayed behind to serve Absalom, what he should do next.

Ahithophel gives him some pretty lurid, jaw-dropping advice.

> *"Have relations with your father's concubines, whom he has left behind to take care of the house; then all Israel will hear that you have made yourself repulsive to your father. The hands of all who are with you will also be strengthened." So, they pitched a tent for Absalom on the roof, and Absalom had relations with his father's concubines in the sight of all Israel.*
> – 2 Samuel 16:21-22

I told you it was racy. I tell you what, though – it's amazing how sin tends to come full circle. David, from that very palace rooftop, had spied a woman named Bathsheba washing herself, and in secret, he stole her, had his way with her, had her husband killed, and married her to cover his tracks when he found out she was pregnant.

His immorality was secret. His shame was public. And all those poor women got caught in the crossfire. Sin hurts a lot of people, including those doing the sinning.

We can read onward in the next chapter, where Ahithophel continues his advice. He says, 'There's a part 2 to my counsel.'

> *Furthermore, Ahithophel said to Absalom, "Please let me choose twelve thousand men and let me set out and pursue David tonight. And I will attack him while he is weary and exhausted and startle him, so that all the people who are with him will flee. Then I will strike and kill the king when he is alone, and I will bring all the people back to you. The return of everyone depends on the man whom you are seeking; then all the people will be at peace."*
> – 2 Samuel 17:1-3

"Strike now!" Ahithophel is saying. "Finish him off!" Because he knew that David had some practice being on the run. If David were able to regroup and come back, he would eventually emerge victorious.

Ahithophel's advice seemed good to Absalom, but he still wanted to get a second opinion. That second opinion suggested not attacking right away, but instead gathering his forces so that he could hit David full force later on.

Absalom liked this counsel better than what Ahithophel had suggested, so he decided to wait it out.

When Ahithophel hears of this development, he does not take it well.

> *Now when Ahithophel saw that his advice had not been followed, he saddled his donkey and set out and went to his home, to his city, and set his house in order, and hanged himself; so, he died and was buried in his father's grave.*
>
> – 2 Samuel 17:23

Ahithophel knew he was done for. Absalom did not finish the job when he had the chance, so he knew that David would eventually come back and punish his betrayers. He felt that he might as well end his own life.

What a strange story, right?

It gets even stranger. But, like sin does, it comes full circle, and it ties in with the bitterness and anger we've been talking about.

David seems to write about this advice of Ahithophel in Psalm 55:

> *For it is not an enemy who taunts me, then I could endure it; nor is it one who hates me who has exalted himself against me, then I could hide myself from him. But it is you, a man my equal, my companion and my confidant; we who had sweet fellowship together, walked in the house of God among the commotion.*
>
> – Psalm 55:12-14

Ahithophel was David's close friend and advisor for many years. Why would he stay behind and help David's rebellious son? Why would he give such disgusting and shameful advice? And why did he go off and kill himself?

Never let anyone tell you that genealogies are boring in scripture. We get all sorts of incredible details in there. For our purposes, we can see from 2 Samuel 23:34 that Ahithophel had a son named Eliam. In 2 Samuel 11:3, we learn that Eliam had a daughter.

That daughter's name was Bathsheba.

That's right, Ahithophel was grandfather to the woman that David stole away from her husband and rushed into a new marriage. He killed Ahithophel's grandson-in-law. He made a mockery of Ahithophel's family, and for 11 years, Ahithophel burned with secret rage. A true Mountain of Bitterness.

That rage finally got an outlet when he told Absalom to rape all of David's concubines, and when Ahithophel took his own life.

Did Ahithophel have a right to be angry at David? Of course, he did! But, as far as we know, he did not confront David – who repented and wept over his sin with Bathsheba and may have been receptive to Ahithophel, his friend. He let the anger simmer inside of him, and when it blew out of him a decade later, it caused horrible death, destruction, and pain.

Forgiveness before God like David was given doe does not mean the persons wronged have also forgiven. We see in this true event that there are consequences to bad actions.

Bitterness never ends well. Revenge is never worth it.

Bitterness strikes when you allow hurt to become hate. You poke it and stroke it, and you feed it, and you fan it, and you stir up the flames to try and relieve the pain of your hurt, but bitterness can never heal.

Only God can heal. And the way He heals in us, is forgiveness.

David did pay the price for his sin. Ahithophel paid for his sin that came out of bitterness.

Nobody ever gets away with anything.

So let God be the judge. Your job is to forgive and trust God with the justice part of your hurt. In His grace, God has allowed us 12 hours of anger, max.

But that's it. If the sun goes down and you're still dwelling on anger, you are in sin. Learn to forgive easily, often, and sincerely, and the journey of faith will open up before you. Move the mountain of bitterness in your life today, if need be, take ownership of the problems and pray that mountain away.

Chapter 6

Healing Through Faith Conflicts

In 2021 and 2022, a podcast called "The Rise and Fall of Mars Hill" came out from Christianity Today, chronicling the birth, growth, and sudden death of one of the largest non-denominational churches in the history of our country. The show has its pros and cons, but one thing that it does an excellent job of is showing how people can get chewed up and spit out by a church, or spiritually abused by pastors. This podcast caught on because it resonated with a lot of people in an area that we aren't always comfortable talking about:

Sometimes you get hurt by the church. And man, is it easy to get bitter, isolated, and angry when that happens.

Judy and I served in some great churches. One being First Baptist Church Cary. It was one of our most fruitful and blessings to us personally. Our girls loved it and to this day we have lifelong friendships. Sadly, the pastor and deacons were at war our entire time and the church actually went through a split. Being the student minister at a large church and seeing the adults battle and see the youth group grow is not normal. We were able to see healing before, during and after the split. I stayed friends with Pastor Steve even after he and many of my friends left to plant a new work. You see it was Steve that got me hooked on Harley's. Steve was an amazing preacher. He followed a long-term Pastor of nearly thirty years and bottom line is the old guard would not accept him. We had over 40 active deacons and six full time ministers, a dozen other staff and interns. (We even had a paid nurse and cook). This church was mission minded and gospel centered. They could just not accept the leadership style change. How do you heal wounded believers? Sharon Jackson was one of the lady deacons and she would weep, read passages, and beg for peace among the mostly male deacon body. Even splits in a church moving some one way and others staying is not healing. Too many Christians are not willing to yield to their pride and selfish preferences. Let's talk more about healing.

A friend of mine has a house on the beach, and he is sure to always keep sheets of plywood handy, as well as a fully charged drill. Why? Because it's not a question of, "Will a storm come?" It is a question of, "When is the storm going to come?" In recognizing the inevitable, it's good to be prepared.

Conflict between believers or conflict inside of a church is going to happen. It's not if but when. That doesn't mean we have to be ruined by it, and it certainly doesn't mean we need to descend into bitterness and fall off the path of faith.

A good church can change a whole city. I've seen it happen a number of times. But we will rub up against others in church who act out of their sin or brokenness and cause more hurt. Or sometimes a man will be put in charge of pastoring a church because he is charismatic and a talented speaker, but instead of carrying forth the mission of God, all he cares about are the ABC's:

- Attendance
- Baptisms
- Cash

For most, the church is a tremendous blessing, I believe. But we want to make sure that for those who have been hurt by the church, that we recognize them, that we see their wounds, and that we do whatever we can to help them heal.

Because even while broken systems need to be fixed, bad leaders need to be set to the side, and offenses need to be reconciled, what is most important for you and I on an individual level is that we do not allow circumstances or trials to make us bitter.

See, if the devil can't drag your soul to hell, the next best thing he can do is neutralize you. He can make you totally preoccupied and ineffective for God's Kingdom.

It looks something like this: AAA.

No, I'm not talking about the auto insurance company. The three "A's" are the process of being taken out of the fight. Someone in the church hurts you somehow, then you get:

Angry.

If you do not deal with that anger, address the problem and try to fix it, or at minimum find it in your heart to forgive, then you will inevitably move onto the second A:

Apathy.

"Why should I help with the mission trip? They play favorites when divvying up the roles."

"Why should I donate money to the church's benevolence fund? The pastor said something rude to me."

"Why should I show up on Sunday morning if they mishandled that situation with my friend?"

Stewing on that anger makes you depressed and apathetic. You don't want to participate in the life of the community, because we tend to withdraw when we are hurting. Eventually, you slide into the final A:

Absence.

You just aren't part of the fight anymore, at a certain point. You got mad, then you got apathetic, and now it's been six months since you've showed up, you don't talk with any of your old friends from the church except to complain about the church, and you're missing out on the guidance, teaching, and charitable works that the church is doing together.

The devil would much, much rather we all go off and be a bunch of lone rangers with our faith, because we are far more effective when we work together.

But angry, apathetic, and alone? Those are the devil's favorite kind of Christians. The ones that are MIA – missing in action.

We even see an example of bitterness between fellow members of the church in the Bible, and it caused division and trouble for a while.

In the Book of Acts, we see Paul the apostle and his mentor Barnabas do incredible missionary work together. They spread the gospel to people who have never heard it before, they fought for the oppressed and downtrodden, they met the needs of the poor, and they even cleaned up some pretty messy situations to help get people back on track.

But then, there was an offence.

A young believer named John Mark decided to leave from one of their missions when he should not have. Maybe he was a young hothead. Maybe he didn't realize the hurt he would cause by leaving Paul in the lurch. Whatever it was, it caused a rift, because, from the look of it, Paul didn't really want to forgive him for what he'd done. At minimum, Paul didn't want to let John Mark participate in ministry with him anymore, but Barnabas disagreed. He wanted to disciple John Mark and give him another chance, but their disagreement was so sharp that Paul and Barnabas had to part ways.

The dynamic duo of the early church broke apart because of hurt from within the Body of Christ, and an unwillingness to reconcile.

Paul the apostle was an incredible person, I think you'd agree. But even he could fall prey to this sort of temptation. When you or I are hurt by the church, it has an added layer of intensity, because the church is where we've been healed before. It's full of people who are supposed to love us and act like Jesus. When someone does something sinful against us, the hurt is that much greater, because all people, members of (and leaders of) the church should be doing the right thing.

Thankfully, there is a happy ending to the story of Paul and John Mark. Paul writes well of him in his later letters, and it seems that they did eventually reconcile and restore John Mark to the work of the Gospel. Eventually, John Mark went on to collaborate with Peter and wrote the Gospel of Mark, which we believe to be the oldest gospel account in the Bible.

Hurt from the church does happen sometimes. Wrongs need to be righted. Destructive leaders need to be removed. And we can take some courage in the fact that the church does police itself eventually.

But we still have to forgive. Occasionally, you need to find a new church if the culture is toxic. But don't let the devil trick you into dropping out. God has a place for you. He has a plan for you. And He doesn't want you to be isolated from your brothers and sisters in the Lord who ought to minister to you, be ministered to by you, and labor next to you.

SECTION II: *Moving the Mountain of Bitterness*

If you leave the best thing is to be kind. Barnabas and Paul had a parting of the ways over John Mark. They were more effective at this point apart than together. They chose peace and we should too.

Wounds come in various types and sizes. Some people get offended theologically, or they get treated unfairly, or any number of other offenses can happen. What matters most is that we are seeking healing together.

Matthew 18, in which Jesus discusses church discipline and reconciliation, is a very misinterpreted verse, in my opinion. Sometimes, to follow the Bible's advice, people just end up beating up on each other. But the point is not to win the argument, it is to win against your brother.

So, when you have an offense with somebody –

Step 1 – Go to them directly.

So many problems can be avoided by just addressing them out in the open. Sometimes what seems like a malicious act is just unawareness of your need or perspective. Don't assume the worst. Go to your pastor, volunteer coordinator, fellow church-member – whoever it is who has hurt you – and diplomatically lay it all out.

Step 2 – Find a mutually agreeable mediator.

This step is where a lot of people go wrong. "Bring another along with you" in Matthew 18 can turn into people finding someone who already agrees with them to go and beat up on the person you're offended with. Instead, if there is a rift between you and someone else, look for a mediator, not backup. Have you and the person who's hurt you both explain your sides of the story, and hopefully the mediator can bring insight and clarity – maybe even a whole solution.

Step 3 – Bring it before the church.

This is only in extreme cases. But even here, I think the previous mediator ought to speak based on his findings. Then the matter can be judged fairly. If anyone owes an apology, the church can direct them. If restitution is owed, it can be settled. Or, if someone really isn't willing to reconcile, at least you have done your best to work it out, and you can let go of bitterness. It's on them, now, and you don't have to feel like you need to leave the whole church behind.

In all of this, our goal is to shrink the conflict, not to grow it. So, remember that the Book of James instructs us to be swift to listen, slow to speak, and slow to anger. The family of God ought to be good at conflict resolution and restoration. That's the idea, anyway. Be a force for good in your congregation, instead of just letting resentment and bitterness stew in you, taking you out of the fight.

We must keep things in proportion.

When someone is hurt by a pastor, sadly, they sometimes decide that all pastors are untrustworthy. When someone is hurt by the church, they sometimes decide that all of Christianity is a lie. But the old saying is true: "One bad apple doesn't spoil the whole bunch."

Healing can take some time, by the way. We set ourselves up for failure if we just want to do it like McDonalds (Make it quick and give me my prize, or I'm out!).

I remember one time when I was in seminary, two girls in my youth group were having a big fight. So, I marched them up to the youth room, and said, "No one is leaving here until we figure this out."

I'll spare you the details. It did not go well.

One thing we found out is that the mothers had problems that carried over to their daughters... They allowed bitterness to not only settle in their hearts, but their children and other young people felt a need to pick sides. This is not God's way.

I can laugh about it now, but it was ugly in that room! Their resentments and bitterness went so much deeper than the little issue I thought we'd solve in five minutes. At one point, they both turned on me!

It's ok to go off and pray for a week. Decide to seek healing. Be willing to accept your part in the offense, recognizing that you have faults too, and that may have contributed to the problem.

Splitting off from your church ought to be a last resort. It's not that it isn't ever necessary, in extreme cases, it's that we shouldn't be so quick to leave a faith community where we have invested. It is unfortunate how quick we are to split off and start a church down the road. A lot of this bitterness and division gets obscured under the guise of "church-planting," but starting a new church based off of a seed of bitterness is sure to end badly.

If you must leave, leave graciously, and try not to burn your bridges. People might come around in the future.

Healing is sometimes slow. You may need to find a counselor to help you sort out your feelings or to process what happened. Do a lot of praying. Forgive as quickly as you are able.

Because, at the end of the day, we do need one another. Most conflicts aren't worth holding grudges over. And whenever the devil wants to stop a good work, he's going to try and get Christians offended at one another.

I'll leave you with this final thought:

A strong draft horse, when harnessed, can pull 8,000lbs behind it. That's incredible. But how much weight do you suppose two draft horses can pull when harnessed together?

You'd be tempted to say 16,000lbs, since each horse can pull 8,000lbs, but this is not the case. Two draft horses, pulling together, can drag 24,000lbs, and, if trained specifically to work together, they can drag 32,000lbs – four times as much as each horse could pull on its own.

Your efforts, when combined with mine, do not yield twice the result. Our efforts do not add together.

They multiply.

In the next section, I'm going to tell a few unflattering stories that take place among people in various churches I've worked in over the years. I won't name any names, and I'm not bringing these stories up to be spiteful – they make a point that is important for us to make. But I want you to keep in mind what we've meditated on in this chapter:

Someone doing church wrong doesn't mean that church is bad; it means that what's wrong ought to be fixed. So, let's be God's hands and feet as we work out our lives together, in His community of believers.

Section II: Summary

How to Move the Mountain of Bitterness

- Resentment, grudges, and bitterness are only natural. But God invites us to partake of the supernatural. That means forgiveness.

- Bitterness is like poisoning your morning cup of coffee, drinking it, and hoping someone else dies.

- God can bring goodness out of difficulty if we continue on the path of faith.

- You are not allowed to hold onto anger for longer than 12 hours. Figure out how to make peace in your heart before you go to bed.

- Conflict, offense, and hurt will happen. Not "if" but "when." So be prepared to walk through them graciously.

- The three A's that take us out: Anger, Apathy, Absence (MIA).

- It is easier to forgive when we remember that God has forgiven us.

- We can accomplish exponentially more together than separately.

SECTION III:

Dealing with the Mountain of Division

Chapter 7

Faith Fixing Solutions

My older sister Michele was my best friend growing up, but at times she was my archrival. She and I could fight over the littlest of issues, and boy, could she lay a punch. But, despite getting on each other's nerves on occasion, we were always loyal to one another. We knew we were family.

One day after elementary school, two boys pinned me to the wall and were about to beat me up. Then one of their friends came running up and said, "Are you guys crazy?" One of the bullies said, "No, I am about to beat up this little punk." Then his friend said, "Do you know who his big sister is? Michele Duncan!!"

Both bullies apologized to me and ran off, never to be seen again. You see, my sister liked to play football with the boys, tackle, and all, and she took no prisoners. Yes, as tough as she was on the outside, she was very kindhearted on the inside and loyal. Fast forward to college and my best friend Doug Hinshaw was on a date with a girl. I was not with him, but Doug upset a group of boys, and they surrounded him, about to beat him up. Doug tells me it was like Moses parting the red sea when Michele came barreling through the crowd, pushing the boys aside and pointing in their faces and chests saying, "This is my brother's friend, and if you try to hurt him, then you have to go through me." She was dating one of the star-running backs on the football team, and let's just say they all got in their cars and let Doug live to see another day.

My sister bought me my first study bible, Ryrie, and when my high school friends took that vow of silence against me, it was my sister that was a true friend, prayer warrior, and confidant. We were quite a faith team in our youth group. You see, it is important to stick together, even in tough times. The devil loves division. He led the first split ever recorded when he took 1/3 of the angels from God's presence.

Jesus famously said that a kingdom divided against itself cannot stand, and He was right. When we fight, grumble, selfishly compete with one another, split off, and complain, God's kingdom work isn't going to be getting done. Not only that, we ourselves, as well as our communities, will be miserable. God has a better way.

Division in the church is so ugly when it's unresolved, there is always a solution. Resolution is a beautiful thing, and it's amazing to watch how God can put the broken pieces together to form a new, thriving community of saints.

Let me tell you a story:

Relaunching a church that has split multiple times and has had numerous, messy changeups in leadership is never your first job choice. Even still, when Apison Baptist Church, a church I had served at as Youth Minister years before, called me to inquire about hiring me, I took the meeting. I didn't want to take the meeting, but I felt like the Lord was leading me to hear them out.

They were not in a happy situation. The church was down to 28 attendees on a Sunday morning, and exactly half of these were to leave shortly after, when the music pastor left to go to another church.

But I'm getting ahead of myself. To really understand how things were, you would have had to be at the Cracker Barrel with the search committee and me, a few weeks before they voted to hire me to pastor the church.

Not knowing who we were, I asked our waitress when she came to the table if she could recommend a church for me, as I was thinking of moving to the area. She recommended her church first, but I specified that I'd like to find a church in Apison. She said that she could not think of a church to recommend.

I said, "What about Apison Baptist? Have you heard of them? I think I saw a sign on my way here."

She scrunched up her face and said, "Don't go there! All they do is fight."

This was in front of the entire search committee. She left, everyone hung their heads, and I said, "You needed to hear that. I think you guys know that we've got some work to do."

SECTION III: *Dealing with the Mountain of Division*

And they did know. They had been humbled. So, despite the division, their hearts were prepared to let the Lord heal and bring them together again. Now it was my turn, and my wife's turn, to respond.

Judy and I prayed about the opportunity, and we decided that we would answer the call.

For eight weeks we had meetings talking about problems and solutions. At the end of it, I handed them this graphic that I had come up with:

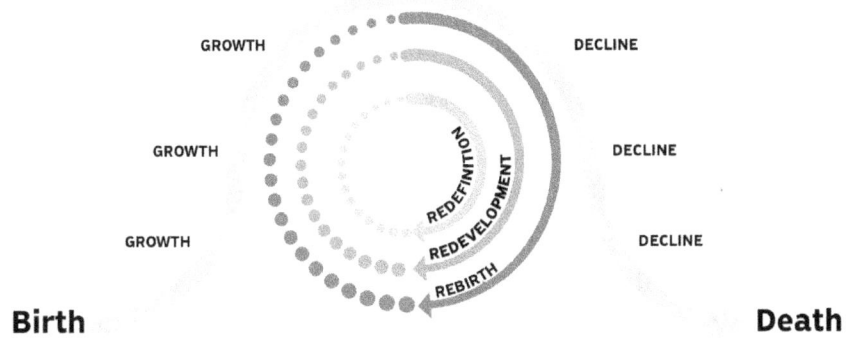

Reference: Baltimore-Washington UMC Conference, bwcumc.org

The idea was that all institutions have a life cycle. They are born, they grow, they mature into something stable, but then, after a while, they decline until they finally cease to exist. But not all institutions last the same amount of time. Some are able to keep to their core mission while reinventing themselves from time to time. Our church was deeply divided and near "death." So, our first step was to redefine who we were, how we would move forward, and what our mission was.

Our purpose statement is:

"Taking Jesus as He is to people as they are."

We prayed and fasted. We saw a glimpse of God's heart of compassion for those who are lost, struggling, confused, or in need. We grew a desire to redefine our community from something that just happens on Sunday morning, to a group of people making positive change in the world around us Monday – Saturday. Sunday was a day of rest.

This was huge for us to overcome division. Now, the Sunday meeting, while important, was not the main focus, and our own particular desires and needs were not center stage. We defined ourselves as existing to serve others in the name of Christ, and that had profound effects on us.

Instead of counting noses on Sunday, we wanted to know how many people we could bless all week long.

With our vision fixed, we were ready to move to the green circle in the chart: redevelopment.

Now that we had redefined, we needed to organize ourselves to accomplish the new vision. We took over the operation of a local food pantry, which is open 7 days a week, and we feed 1,200 families each month. That's 3,000 plus individuals.

We have a homeless ministry, where we take resource bags and other supplies to the unhoused. We talk with them, feed them, and pray for them.

Once a church that fought constantly even within its own doors, now we partner with six churches, all from different denominations, as well as several independent Bible Study groups, and numerous grocery stores and local farms (for our campaigns to feed the hungry.)

We have people who voted for Trump and people who voted for Biden working side by side with smiles on their faces. We have vaccinated and unvaccinated. Old and young. Introverts and extroverts. We're all united.

How is this possible? Because we have redefined ourselves, redeveloped into a church that is focused on a common work that we can do together, and because God gave new life to our community.

We experienced rebirth.

Our church is still not a large one. We aren't trying to be. But we punch above our weight, so to speak, by the grace of God, and we impact a lot of lives each week. That's why my wife calls us "Gideon's army."

We were tested during the COVID lockdowns, but we hung together and kept doing the Lord's work, we did not shut down. Later, in a radio interview, I was asked why we did not shut down our church or our food pantry when most everyone else did.

My answer goes back to what I asked our church on my first Sunday as pastor:

SECTION III: *Dealing with the Mountain of Division*

"If this church shut down and ceased to exist, would the community mourn our absence."

By the time the COVID lockdowns hit, the answer was "yes." People depended on us. We were finally hitting our stride. You see, the church had almost shut down due to so many internal conflicts, and I could not see a sudden end imposed on that new life. We declared, "This is our time to shine in the midst of the tragedy," and we did just that.

The interview went so well they offered me a one-day radio show, and because the ratings from that were so high, they offered me a daily show. Now I have been moved for the drive-home traffic, 3-6 pm on NOOGA Radio Network, broadcasting into multiple stations in Tennessee, Georgia, Kentucky, New Jersey, and Alabama. The Macil Duncan Show is also on Facebook, Truth Social and Rumble.

The show has allowed me to reach people all over the world, literally, and we have received funds from many states to help us feed the hungry. Many go online at www.ApsionBaptist.com and go to the giving options to help us meet many needs.

All the sudden, our church was no longer a source of division, but a nexus, a center point of connection for people trying to do God's work. We were able to Move the Mountain of Disagreement.

What a beautiful turnaround.

Another area that God blessed was our Operation Christmas Child ministry. Like most churches we did the fall drives and made 75-100 boxes. Well, our children's church leader, Lisa G., decided to become a year-round coordinator right before COVID hit.

One store got a double order of supplies when all the other shipments were stuck at sea. We were the only pantry open, so we picked up what they wanted to donate, and six trips later our gymnasium was packed. Then, we were able to let our brand-new OCC Coordinator fill up her supply closet we had just designated, and we did over 300 boxes.

There were enough supplies left over for a food pantry fundraiser, and after that we had so much stuff our new AWANA Director filled her AWANA store, and we still had two pickup trucks and a trailer load of new items to give to a sister church to help them with a sale. You see, having faith of a mustard seed and staying open also impacted many other ministries. But it was only possible because a) we still existed and b) we were working together.

August 2023 starts my seventh year here at Apison Baptist Church. We have been given two first place awards for baptisms by our local association and have been blessed with many new families moving here from California, Illinois, New York, and Georgia.

Six years ago, if you had told me all this and so much more would have happened, I would have laughed. But the Lord can take the faith of a mustard seed and bless it to bless thousands. With the church, pantry, radio, and media we are feeding thousands, which was well beyond our imagination. God gets all the glory!

Allow me to drive the point home one last time:

If we were still fighting, if we had allowed the church to die, if we had not forgiven and reoriented ourselves outward, to do God's work, there would be many more hungry people, many more lonely people on the street, and a lot of kids without Christmas boxes.

Unity is not just so that you and I feel comfortable. Working together can be uncomfortable at times. But while the world tells us, "Split off if you can't work together," by faith, we are laboring to become one in Christ.

The results speak for themselves.

The in-fighting and splitting off that the church had experienced is one kind of division, but there are others. Sometimes there is a generation gap within a church. Sometimes there is division over politics. And sometimes, unfortunately, I've seen racial division.

And man, there's just nothing quite so ugly as that.

Because when Jesus was asked what the greatest commandment was, He responded this way:

> *And He said to him, "'You shall love the Lord your God with all your heart, and with all your soul, and with all your mind.' This is the great and foremost commandment. The second is like it, 'You shall love your neighbor as yourself.' Upon these two commandments hang the whole Law and the Prophets."*
>
> *– Matthew 22:37-40*

If you had to sum up the whole Bible in one word, it would be "Love." So, we always need to check ourselves and make sure that we are sharing the love of God with others.

When we do not, division rises like a mountain in our path.

> *We count those blessed who endured. You have heard of the patience of Job and have seen the outcome of the Lord's dealings, that the Lord is full of compassion and is merciful.*
>
> – James 5:11

I saw faith undo evil and bring healing and unity. After seminary, for example, I planted a church in Mississippi, and we had to move locations 13 times because we kept growing. We met in a library, an auto auction, hotel ball room, ... wherever we could fit. We didn't have a lot of resources, but God was working, and there was always a way forward.

A man named Eric Boon, an AME pastor nearby, ended up letting us use their church for an early morning service, while his church came in and ministered at 11 o'clock. We'd host pulpit swaps, teach each other's congregations from time to time, and we did a lot of good work together – and Eric and I became great friends, besides.

That's what faith can do in the face of division. What the devil meant for evil, God will use for good if you walk the path of faith.

Chapter 8

How Not to Stumble

2 Peter 1:1-10 tells us there are seven things that if you "PRACTICE," you will not stumble.

> *Simon Peter, a bondservant and apostle of Jesus Christ, to those who have received a faith of the same kind as ours, by the righteousness of our God and Savior, Jesus Christ: Grace and peace be multiplied to you in the knowledge of God and of Jesus our Lord, for His divine power has granted to us everything pertaining to life and godliness, through the true knowledge of Him who called us by His own glory and excellence. Through these He has granted to us His precious and magnificent promises, so that by them you may become partakers of the divine nature, having escaped the corruption that is in the world on account of lust. Now for this very reason also, applying all diligence, in your faith supply moral excellence, and in your moral excellence, knowledge, and in your knowledge, self-control, and in your self-control, perseverance, and in your perseverance, godliness, and in your godliness, brotherly kindness, and in your brotherly kindness, love. For if these qualities are yours and are increasing, they do not make you useless nor unproductive in the true knowledge of our Lord Jesus Christ. For the one who lacks these qualities is blind or short-sighted, having forgotten his purification from his former sins. Therefore, brothers and sisters, be all the more diligent to make certain about His calling and choice of you. For as long as you practice these things, you will never stumble.*
>
> – 2 Peter 1:1-10, emphasis added.

Have you ever heard of a tent revival?

It's where you get a big tent, hook up a sound system, and invite as many people as you can get your hands on to come out and hear the gospel. Out here in the South, we have lots of tent revivals. In fact, sometimes the summer months are called "revival season."

Now, these events can be powerful, and I had the opportunity, as a seminary student, to go and preach to the youth at a large tent revival in Texas, while a well-known preacher took the big meetings.

There are an awful lot of good people in God's church; don't misunderstand me, but there is a contingent of preachers that care less about the gospel and more about the ABC's.

That'd be attendance, baptisms, and cash, as you'll recall from a previous chapter.

The evangelist at this week-long tent was Sam Cathy. He was funny and charismatic. He was a busy man that week and we never got to really talk. He was upset that no one had given their life to Christ.

By the Lord's grace, I was having a different experience, in that all week we had been going to FCA groups, morning bible studies at local schools, prayer groups, sports practices at many area schools. We quickly began to see the fruit of the youth pastors and myself spending mornings and afternoons meeting the teenagers on their turf. I spent all week with these kids, and the Spirit was doing a work. By the end of the week, we had a Youth Night with nearly 800 students attending. I gave a gospel invitation and 136 kids responded to a salvation message. The main evangelist heard about these numbers, and he sent a messenger to tell me to bring all these kids into the main tent, to march them in front of the crowd.

I told the messenger that I didn't want to pull these new Christian kids away from their counselors, as older believers explained the basics of the faith to them.

After the service I went over to a Pizza Restaurant which was closing, seeing me coming with about 30-40 students behind me and more behind them they locked the door. An employee allowed me to come in but locked the door behind us and he explained that closing was 15-20 minutes, and they just could not facilitate this large crowd since they sent some server's home. I said, "That's fine, I understand. May I share the good news with you?"

I got a look that can only be described as befuddled, and the kids outside, looking through the window, started whispering amongst themselves.

See, the young man I was talking with who worked at the pizza place was a skinhead. He was all tatted up. And, apparently, he had a reputation for being a mean son of a gun, and a bigot, to boot. The kids were afraid of him.

But I didn't know any of that. Sometimes it's better not to know what you're up against. He said I had till they closed. I opened up a New Testament and shared the Roman road with him. He shared with me he had never heard that before.

He could not believe that a God could love him. He got down on his knees with me and prayed the sinner's prayer and wept. He was convicted and broken.

This was a true God moment. All the students that had walked over were watching through the window. They had just witnessed 136 saved at the Youth Night but this seemed to be more impressive. As I went outside the students all knew this young man and that he was bully troublemaker at their high school. No doubt that Jesus brought us together, and more importantly, it reconciled that skinhead with all the kids who were afraid of him. So, ego brings division, but Jesus unifies the brethren.

If I had taken the 136 kids over to the big tent to show them off to the adults, then I would have missed this gospel opportunity.

Nobody had to parade him around or anything.

The reason I bring all of this up is because there are going to be disagreements amongst brothers and sisters in the Lord, but the journey of faith requires that we deal with division – and overcome it! And thankfully, the Bible gives us some instruction on how to do that.

The best way to avoid a black eye is to avoid getting into a fight, so in this chapter, we're going to discuss the Bible's ideas on how to prepare and defend against division, so that you don't stumble so much in the first place. In the next chapter, we'll talk more about what to do when division arises.

As we opened this chapter with 2 Peter 1:1-10 we are told if we practice living certain parts of scripture that we will not stumble!

The apostle Peter, in 2 Peter 1:5-8, gives us an incredible chain of character traits to help us avoid stumbling. It goes something like this:

- First, you start with faith.

- Then add moral excellence to that.

- Then add knowledge.

- Empowered with knowledge, exercise self-control.

- When exercising self-control, persevere.

- Let godliness come out of that perseverance.

- Godliness should grow into brotherly kindness, so cultivate it.

- And finally, in brotherly kindness, learn what it really means to love.

The longer you meditate on these seven virtues and then decide to practice them, the more impact the Word has in your life. Peter is promising you will not stumble.

We can't start being perfect all of the sudden. Nobody is perfect aside from Jesus anyway, but as we try to learn how to imitate him, there are baby steps to take.

All you need to start is a little bit of faith. Mustard seed size can move your mountain if you believe but as Peter tells us practice being godly.

We must practice moral excellence. Simply trying to live honestly, working hard, telling the truth, and keeping your nose clean will take you another step toward love.

We have a great number of people in this country that know we ought to be loving others, but they have no idea what Jesus taught about love, or how God loves His people. How can your moral excellence really stand up, past a certain point, if you don't even know the Ten Commandments?

As Voddie Bachham asks, "By what standard?"

We need to learn and internalize God's standards – what He says is good and just – and then we can make that moral excellence in our faith complete.

Once we have some knowledge, it's going to take self-control to stick to what we've learned. Practicing that is going to develop patience. And patient suffering truly is the breeding ground for godly character.

SECTION III: *Dealing with the Mountain of Division*

Many of us actually pray harder, seek deeper in the bible and try to live more holy when we are being persecuted. God allows tough times it seems so we will be forced to practice the principles of His Word.

Allen Iverson famously made fun of practice while he was in the NBA. He was fined for skipping or being late to practice. He had a news conference to say he was one of the best players in the league and he did not need to practice.

Many Christians are like Allen Iverson, no need to be active in church, small group, daily devotions, and prayer. They wonder why they stumble into sin, allow bad people or habits into their lives.

The key to enduring a hard time, persevering in your self-control regardless of the obstacles: Trust that the pain isn't for no reason. Trust that God is doing a good work in you, and it'll turn into godliness if you let Him do what He does.

As we imitate Jesus, learning godliness, it's going to turn our eyes to the people around us. We'll be understanding with their weakness because God has been understanding with our weakness. So, we learn to be kind to one another because God is kind.

It's not much farther from there to love, and always remember:

Love is the destination.

God is love. Anyone who dwells in love dwells in God, as 1 John says. And if you live in love, you're not going to let your church divide over nonsense. You're not going to let a small offense turn into a big ordeal.

What's even better is, if you and the others in your church community are steadily practicing Peter's list of virtues, then you'll avoid drifting away from one another over meaningless fights and ego trips.

We need to make it a spiritual practice to inspect our lives from time to time and see where we are on the list. What do you need to work on? Present your efforts to the Lord in glad response to the kindness He has shown you.

I wish that were the end of it. I wish I could tell you that people's egos are the only problem causing division in and out of the church, but I can't. There really is such a thing as the devil, and a church may as well have a big red and white target on the roof, as far as spiritual warfare is concerned. Sometimes the devil and his minions stir up trouble, and we need to be ready for that, too.

Paul provides us with helpful words of wisdom with a present-day metaphor using the most powerful army and solid uniform at the time to express we are powerful soldiers of the Lord!

> *Put on the full armor of God, so that you will be able to stand firm against the schemes of the devil. For our struggle is not against flesh and blood, but against the rulers, against the powers, against the world forces of this darkness, against the spiritual forces of wickedness in the heavenly places.*
>
> – Ephesians 6:11-12

Whoa!

I don't know about you, but when I read that, I get images of a spiritual battleground, with flak exploding in the air, bullets flying, and angels ducking for cover. What are these rulers, powers, and world forces of darkness? What does it mean that there are "spiritual forces of wickedness in the heavenly places?"

It means that the demons know God is going to punish them eternally, but that won't happen until He's done with all His work here. So, wherever a Christian is out there doing the Lord's business, he's going to be a target, because the devil is desperately trying to buy time. He knows he's a condemned, convicted enemy, awaiting his sentence.

Satan doesn't like you very much. He dislikes the brotherly kindness and love in your life even less.

Christians need to gear up for the assault. You aren't worried about stray bullets if you're sitting in a tank, but if you're naked on the battlefield, you're just plain out of luck.

Here's what the apostle Paul says we need to do:

> *Therefore, take up the full armor of God, so that you will be able to resist on the evil day, and having done everything, to stand firm.*
>
> – Ephesians 6:13

Then, he gives us the armor of God.

- *Belt your waist with truth.*

If you don't know who the enemy is, what you're fighting for, or how to do battle, you're going to have a bad time in this war. God's word ties it all together. And, to go with the metaphor, a belt is what you hang your weapons on. Food for thought.

– *Put on the breastplate of righteousness!*

A breastplate is the big piece of armor that goes on your chest and torso. It's the piece of armor that's going to absorb the majority of the damage, and it protects your heart.

There is much to be said for living an upright, upstanding life. It's just plain harder for the devil to take you out if you won't do anything wrong! Learn what righteousness is according to God and live that way. You'll be prepared when the attacks come.

– *Strap the preparation of the gospel of peace on your feet!*

That wording may sound a little funny, but it's how the Bible puts it, so I want to be faithful to what it says. We can break it down.

Be in peace and be ready to share God's message of peace. Doesn't the Book of Proverbs say that a soft answer turns away wrath? I can tell you stories about refusing to fight and offering peace in the face of someone else's anger can take the vinegar right out of them. Be ready to give grace and peace when the way of the world starts swinging. God can use that.

But (and always remember this) how can you be an agent of peace if you do not have peace in your heart? Seek God, and learn how to walk without anxiety or fear, trusting in God.

See, that's what makes you stable. There are a lot of broken shards of glass, shrapnel, rocks, and you name it on a battlefield. Can you imagine being barefoot? You'd be staring at the ground every time you took a step, and you'd no doubt step on something that throws you off balance.

Being in the Lord's peace is like wearing shoes, so you don't get thrown off by every little thing. It steadies you. It makes you ready, ironically, for war. But we wage war with peace, love, and truth.

Fighting fire with fire will only get you so far. I believe that Jesus would have us fight fire with water.

- *Take up the shield of faith!*

Paul says the shield of faith will allow you to "extinguish the flaming arrows of the evil one." So, when trouble comes, even from far off, you know who you are, what path you're walking, and Who God is. Let our faith go before you always, and you will find shelter in the storm.

- *Take the helmet of salvation and the sword of the Spirit, which is the word of God!*

You're already saved if you've trusted in Jesus! That covers your head. No kill shots. So, you're free to take up God's word and do some damage for the Kingdom. Learn what God has said, live by it, cling to it, and you can bring light and life where the devil wants to sow death and division.

This is a point I can't stress enough. Fight by following Jesus. It's the solution to all of the troubles we come up against. And that sword of the spirit will cut through the bleakest, darkest night.

If we walk the journey from faith to love, and wear the armor of God, no foe – either human or spirit – can divide us.

Jesus prayed that we would be one as He and the Father are one. It's time that we take that prayer seriously.

At our food pantry ministry, we work with 7 different denominations. We disagree about the End Times. We don't worship the same way. But we all agreed to follow Jesus, and He told us to serve the poor. That makes us allies.

In Christ, we're one.

Don't ever let anyone tell you different.

Chapter 9

Serve and Overcome

"If Apison Baptist Church ceased to exist, would the community weep our absence?"

This was the question that I asked our church when I took over as lead pastor. At the time, truthfully, the answer was probably no. But today, it's a resounding yes.

Why is that?

By the grace of God, we have become a safe haven in our community for the hungry and homeless. Through our food pantry ministry, we feed thousands each week. We've developed relationships with other churches and businesses near us. Our people serve the homeless and give them much needed prayer, guidance, and supplies. During Covid, we were one of the few churches to keep its doors open, and we were there for many people who needed to be in the house of the Lord.

It is no coincidence that we've stopped fighting with each other during the same period that we've really begun serving. Apison Baptist Church used to be so quarrelsome, and everybody seemed to have an issue. There was a lot of drama. But now, we are united, and the change is wonderful.

Apison Baptist has a great Senior Adult core that not only held this church stay together but still have major impact with the new and younger members. When we went from the pews to the padded chairs in the sanctuary, we saw 100% agreement. We went from the older style of music to blending they were on board. Agreeing to put in the new playground and remodeling the buildings and new signs… they were supportive. Leon Bagby is my chairman of deacons and he said to me, "Pastor whatever it takes to reach the young people we will do our best." His wife Freda has gone to be with the Lord but was my biggest fan and had encouraging words and cards for Judy and I. Loving the people that called you as well as the new members may be a balancing act at times, but they all need to buy into the vision of a pastor if possible.

We voted to move from being a consumer church to being a missional church. Our new by-laws reflect this.

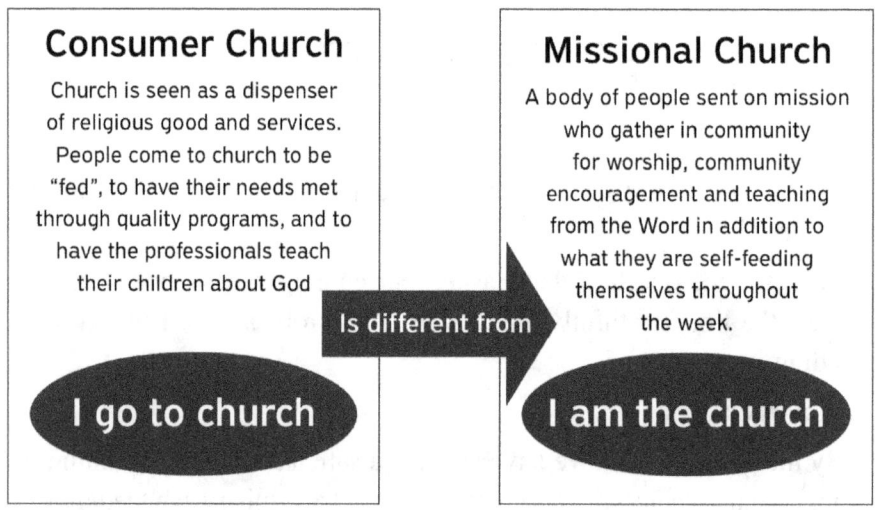

Reference: Gil Rendle, *Back to Zero*

Historically, the church has seen itself as missional. We need to spread the good news of Christ to every corner of the globe, and Jesus instructed us to not only tell the world, but to transform it, teaching the nations to observe all that He commanded.

That's a tall order. We're going to need all the help we can get.

In our consumerist, American culture, we've let ourselves slip into a cruise ship mentality. We think that a Sunday service exists just to cater to our needs. People hop from church to church to find exciting programs, more entertaining sermons, or a bigger coffee bar. But this isn't what Jesus has in mind for His Body to be doing.

> *What is the source of quarrels and conflicts among you? Is the source not your pleasures that wage war in your body's parts?*
>
> – James 4:1

Consumers sit to be served by others. Missional people go to serve others. When we only focus on ourselves, we get division. When we invest in the kingdom of God and serve, we get unity. That's the path of faith.

The Apison Food Pantry is our gift from God so that we can be a giver to the community.

Sometimes we overspiritualize our Christian faith. We have to remember that Jesus spent a lot of His time serving. Jesus healed people just about everywhere He went. He fed the 4,000, and then later he fed the 5,000 somewhere else! The apostle John helps us get our head on straight with this one.

> *But whoever has worldly goods and sees his brother or sister in need, and closes his heart against him, how does the love of God remain in him? Little children, let's not love with word or with tongue, but in deed and truth.*
>
> – 1 John 3:17-18

Serving opens your heart.

One thing that we do at Apison Baptist is "Servant Sunday." On Servant Sunday, we gather together for a song and a short prayer, and then we all go out and do good in the community. It teaches our young people that faith is active, and not just sitting back and absorbing a sermon. There are real people out there that are hurting and need the love of God. Who else is going to give it to them, if not God's people?

We can't stay divided when we turn our hearts to loving others and working to better our community.

Another thing we are doing this fall is something I'm calling "Operation Conversation." Every member of my church and each listener to my radio show is going to be challenged to have 3 significant conversations each week with someone in need. The rules are:

- Let them talk
- Pray with them
- Give them physical help/supplies/food
- Share about Jesus

Jesus said to go and make disciples. The way I see it, everyone in their life should at least disciple one person. Getting saved means that you have submitted to the Lordship of Christ – the same person Who said to make disciples! This is going to require us getting out of our comfort zones. Getting saved isn't just a 'get out of hell free' card. It means we follow Jesus.

And Jesus came to serve.

There is a proverb that says the day of death can be more joyous than a day of birth. This can only happen if that person has spent his or her life serving God and serving others. A selfless, Christ-centered life is the entrance into glory, and that's something to be celebrated.

But it starts today, and it starts with you and me. The apostle Paul says that we were created in Christ for good works. And you'll find, as you lean into the work that God has for you to do, the strife and division dies down.

Thankfully, the Word of God instructs us even further. You can use a screwdriver to pound a nail in, but you'll be more effective and efficient if you use a hammer, and let that screwdriver turn screws instead. In the same way, the church is made up of all sorts of different kinds of people, with different gifts, callings, and talents. You want to try and serve where you can be most effective – while never being too good to roll up your sleeves and jump in on the work.

It pays to know your spiritual gift.

If I can put on my preacher's cap here for a moment, I'd like to clear up some confusion on this issue.

God is in charge of the gifts that He gives. Some, are like appointments, or positions that people can hold. This is what the spiritual gifts passage in Ephesians 4 is about. It explains five offices in the church.

Some gifts that the Lord gives are like miracles – they happen in the moment, and only the Holy Spirit can decide when. This is what the passage in 1 Corinthians 12 is talking about. If God heals someone of cancer, that person has received a gift of healing. The gift of healing does not mean running around healing whoever you want, any time you want.

And still other gifts are more like skills. Some of these gifts may be things you are born with, others can be developed over time with practice. These practical gifts exist to help the church function as a unit, together doing the work of God effectively. This is what the scripture is referring to in Romans 12:4-8.

It's this passage that we're going to focus on for our purposes here. Paul describes the church body as having many parts, and he lists a number of different kinds of gifts that people have, and should exercise, in service to others:

Prophecy

Contrary to popular belief, this doesn't mean telling the future or calling fire down from the heavens. Yes, some prophets in the Bible did those things, but ultimately, prophecy just means "to speak forth." The gift of prophecy means that you have a knack for saying true, and often difficult, things that need to be said. You are a truth-sayer. We need that in the church.

Service

Abraham Lincoln said it perfectly: "God must love the common people, because He made so many of them." Service is probably the most common of the gifts we will discuss here, but that does not mean it has any less honor or is any less necessary than the other gifts. If you get a flat tire and end up on the side of the road, a prophet isn't going to be much help to you. You want someone with practical skills, a willingness to help, and a good heart. The gift of service is a precious gift, because without it, we would not be a church that does anything. Service is the ability and skill to solve problems and provide for practical needs.

Teaching

Some people have a way with words. They can take a difficult idea and reduce it to something that someone else can understand. Teaching is how we pass on not only the fundamentals of the faith.

A word of caution here – I knew a man who thought he was a pretty good teacher, so he volunteered to help out on Sundays at his church. They put him in with the kids, and he was awful at it. So he told me, "I guess I was wrong. I don't have the gift of teaching." I laughed, gave him a slap on the back, and said, "You have the gift of teaching, Greg. You just don't have the gift of teaching kids. Go teach an adult Sunday school class." Some people are gifted at teaching music, or memory verses, or teaching a specific age group, and some people can teach anything. Teaching equips the body with knowledge.

Exhortation

"Exhortation" is a fancy word that just means encouragement and support. This is a gift that takes many different forms, in my opinion. The cheerful person who is always looking on the bright side, making people laugh or smile – to me, that person has the gift of exhortation. Other people use this gift in counseling situations, where they can encourage someone going through a hard time to do the heart-work and healing that needs to be done, to keep persevering, and to overcome. And then there are your garden variety encouragers, who simply see the good in people and lift up their spirits whenever they engage. Exhortation is the gift that keeps us from getting bogged down, and renews our strength.

Giving

Some people aren't good with people, but they are good with money, and they've worked hard to be able to be generous when a need arises, or a good work needs to be funded. Others aren't necessarily wonderful with money, but they have big hearts and are always looking for ways to give things away, to meet needs, and to bless others with gifts. Whatever they do or do not have, givers have a way of making everyone around them richer, and they go above and beyond the call to supply the work of the ministry. It's the gift that keeps on giving.

Leadership

Have you ever heard the phrase, "He's a born leader"? It's true. You can go to a playground or even a nursery and see that there are some kids the others just want to follow around. Some people can't help but be influential, and others, for whatever reason, are appointed to positions of leadership, where their actions set the tone for many other people. Paul encourages leaders to lead with diligence, meaning not to be lazy or to place all of your burdens on the people following you. Leaders ought to take care of the people they are guiding, and take them to a good place. Leadership moves the mission forward.

Mercy

Some have defined the gift of mercy as the ability to detect and minister to those who are in distress. Doctors or missionaries who help the sick have been called "angels of mercy," and that's the sort of thing we're talking about here. If you look around you to see who is broken or suffering, and you bring them comfort, then you have the gift of mercy. Mercy is the consolation to our brokenness in a fallen world.

If you want to deal with the mountain of division, you're going to have to invest in the kingdom of God by serving. It helps to know what you're good at, when you do.

You can find all sorts of spiritual gifts tests online that will ask you a series of questions and then tell you one or two gifts at the end that you probably have. Finding where you fit in the mission of your church, and in your life's mission in general, is a beautiful thing. It's ok if it takes you a while to figure it out. Start serving in any area and see how it works out. If it's a disaster, try something else. There can be some trial and error involved in all of this, and that's just fine. Seek the Lord in prayer as you search out your gifting, and blessings are sure to follow.

When I was young, I used to get "pastor" and "evangelist" on these spiritual gift tests, but as I've gotten older, I've realized that even though I can certainly function in the giftings of an evangelist, I just make a better pastor. I've leaned into that, and I've seen the Lord work through me effectively in this way.

I am a Baptist preacher, and I love the Baptist denomination, but there are two things that we neglect to talk about in our tradition: sex and the Holy Spirit. Unfortunately, this means others will talk about these topics and inform the opinions of our people, and the church often has nothing to say. So allow me to tell you that the Holy Spirit is God. Knowing the Holy Spirit is a deeply important part of the journey of faith.

A well-known minister once said that every morning when you wake up, you ought to say "good morning" to the Holy Spirit, and I think that's a good idea too. It keeps us engaged with Him, aware of Him, and inviting Him into our daily lives.

I believe that each person is given gifts from the Holy Spirit, as well as assignments. Some people use these gifts and carry out these assignments, and some refuse. Think of Jonah, who had a calling on his life, but initially, he ran away from it.

When he relented and did the work that the Spirit had for him to do, using the gifts he had been given, a whole city repented.

Whether Jonah did his assignment reluctantly or not, it was the Holy Spirit doing the work. We need to remember that no matter how big and scary, or small and insignificant, our calling seems to us, it is ultimately the Holy Spirit that is doing the work, and that's why He gets all the glory.

We can't be divided when we are working together. There just isn't enough time. So invest in the kingdom, learn your spiritual gifts, and serve.

Section III: Summary

Dealing with the Mountain of Division

- Division in the Body of Christ can be overcome.

- Dividing ourselves over skin color, music preferences, or comfort is just silly – and often sinful. Examine your heart and learn to love all kinds of people, like Jesus does.

- 2 Peter 1:5-8 gives us a roadmap for how not to stumble. When we are progressing in sanctification, it is harder to divide nonessential issues.

- Put on the full armor of God because the enemy often sows seeds of division. Coming together in love and reconciliation is a battle won in the spiritual realm.

- Serving together makes it more difficult to divide over silly things.

- Go from consumer-minded to missionally-minded.

- Determine where you are gifted, consider taking a spiritual gifts test, and find somewhere to contribute.

- Trial and error are ok when you are figuring out where you fit in the mission. It's worth the growing pains of finding your niche.

- Value one another, as co-laborers in Christ, fellow soldiers on the battlefield.

SECTION IV:

Conquering the Mountain of Fear

Chapter 10

Fear Lies

If you've never heard the song, "Fear is a Liar," by Zach Williams, stick a bookmark in this page, pull up YouTube or Spotify, and give it a listen. It is a wonderful song, and full of helpful reminders for people of faith.

This is the chorus:

> *Fear, he is a liar*
> *He will take your breath*
> *Stop you in your steps*
> *Fear, he is a liar*
> *He will rob your rest*
> *Steal your happiness*
> *Cast your fear in the fire*
> *Because fear, he is a liar.*

Have you ever heard the phrase, "Like a deer in the headlights?" That's how we are when we let fear into us. It paralyzes us. Stops us dead in our tracks. We can be skipping happily along on the journey of faith, even coming right off of a big victory, when the mountain of fear shoots up out of the ground and grinds us to a halt.

"You won't have enough money."

"If you try to love, you'll only get rejected."

"It doesn't matter if you try or not."

"You're going to fail."

"God doesn't really love you."

"There is no rest for you."

And here's the deal, if what we learned in public school is true, then fear is a rational, reasonable response. The secular world says that you are an accident, the product of blind chance, that there is no deeper meaning to your life, that existence is short, violent, and cruel, and that death is the end.

All that sounds like the premise of a psychological horror novel. But the truth is, Stephen King and Lovecraft haven't got anything on Darwin, Freud, Marx, and Nietzsche. Those four very influential men tell a much more frightening story than anything you'll see at the movies or in a book.

When the world does not acknowledge God, doesn't really have an answer for you when you get afraid.

"Believe in yourself," doesn't really cut it, most of the time, does it? Sure, we need to be encouraged, and I'm not saying to doubt yourself, but when you're staring at an empty bank account, an overdue notice on rent, listening to a crying baby in the other room, and coming right off an argument with your spouse – "believe in yourself" falls flat. Fear seems to make a lot more sense.

But God is bigger than all of that. He's got a prescription for the fears that paralyze and plague us. The journey of faith that He has set us on can move that mountain of fear, but we've got to get our minds set on what He says is true, and then we've got to act in faith.

God has many titles in the Bible: King of Kings, Lord of Lords, The Great I Am, God of the Breakthrough, etc. But perhaps one of the most famous is "Emmanuel," which means "God with us."

It's one of the ways we refer to Jesus around Christmastime. "God is with us." Implied in that, the subtext if you will, is the command "do not be afraid."

After all, that's what the angels told to the shepherds in Luke 2 in the Bible. They announced Jesus' birth and told them, "Do not be afraid." If God is with us, why should we worry?

SECTION IV: *Conquering the Mountain of Fear*

The Bible gives us lots of great advice and instruction on this, no matter what we're afraid of:

> *"For this reason, I say to you, do not be worried about your life, as to what you will eat or what you will drink; nor for your body, as to what you will put on. Is life not more than food, and the body more than clothing? Look at the birds of the sky, that they do not sow, nor reap, nor gather crops into barns, and yet your heavenly Father feeds them. Are you not much more important than they? And which of you by worrying can add a single day to his life's span?"*
> – Jesus, Matthew 6:25-27

> *Do not be anxious about anything, but in everything by prayer and pleading with thanksgiving let your requests be made known to God. And the peace of God, which surpasses all comprehension, will guard your hearts and minds in Christ Jesus.*
> – Philippians 4:6-7

> *"Have I not commanded you? Be strong and courageous! Do not be terrified nor dismayed, for the Lord your God is with you wherever you go."*
> – The angel, speaking to Joshua in Joshua 1:9

There are many, many times that the Bible instructs the reader, or a person in a particular story, not to be afraid. In fact, many people say that it's the most repeated command in the whole of the Scriptures. Clearly, it's an important theme for our lives as we follow God.

If we are fearing, we aren't trusting. If we are trusting, we aren't fearing. Faith and fear, in many ways, are opposites.

If you're having trouble with fear, put your faith in God, and watch what He does as you lean into Him and act on that trust. I don't think you'll be disappointed if you keep at it.

But fear is in our DNA. We're imperfect creatures, and the messages we get constantly from our culture and media certainly don't help. I mean, pull up the news on your phone, and tell me that they aren't selling fear and outrage on a daily basis? We're encouraged to be afraid, because people act rashly when they are in fear. Fear is big business.

But God is the author of peace, and I don't think I need to tell you that living in peace is a lot more fulfilling than living in fear.

The fear is so persistent, however, in our flesh, that we can even start to worry and grow fearful on the heels of a great victory! This is why the Bible is always telling us to remember what God has done for us. It's the antidote to the fear that springs up like a weed every time it rains. But by placing our faith in God's goodness, steadiness, and provision, that fear can be cast aside.

Elijah is my favorite example of this in the Bible.

To get us up to speed, the book of 1 Kings in the Old Testament tells us about an incredible person of faith named Elijah. He is a prophet of God in ancient Israel, called to warn Israel of the consequences for turning to pagan gods and worshipping those demons. He urges them to return to following God.

Part of the problem was King Ahab, a terrible, wicked ruler, and his wife Jezebel, who was the high priestess of an ancient, bloody cult of Baal.

But Elijah was like a lion, even when faced with all of this darkness and power. He knew the God that he served.

Elijah prophesied bold against the king, because of the evil that Ahab had done, and because of the wickedness that Israel was doing, following Ahab's example. Elijah told Ahab that it would no longer rain in Israel until he said otherwise, and then he left.

Take a step back and realize how devastating this curse is. Even today, in our modern, industrialized, sophisticated, irrigated economy, we are only a couple of months from starvation if we stopped growing and producing new food. Elijah proclaimed that it would not rain in Israel, thereby making largescale food production impossible. And this didn't last for a month, or two months. It lasted for three and a half years.

When Elijah showed up again, Ahab was, understandable, furious – even though it was Ahab's own wickedness that had caused this calamity. But again, Elijah was bold. He challenged the priests of Baal to a contest on Mt. Carmel, to see who the true God was once and for all. The 800 hundred of pagan priests opposed Elijah, but nothing happened. Elijah challenged them to dig a ditch around the altar and fill it with water and wet the sacrifice to make it a true miracle to light a fire. They took the challenge.

The last of any water reserves were placed on the altar in an action of faith that God would deliver in the most difficult way. Then Elijah prayed, and fire fell from heaven to consume his offering and the water. And then he prayed again for the rain, and it rained torrentially.[6] The faith of Elijah was strong enough to help the fellow Israelites to pour their precious water believing God would come through. Is your faith contagious? Inspirational to others?

What faith! What courage! This guy's trust in God is phenomenal. But keep reading – only a short while later, Elijah despairs. He becomes fearful that Queen Jezebel is going to hunt him down and kill him. He worries that he is the last of God's servants alive, and that he, too, will soon be dead, and with him, God's mission on earth will be dead, too.

At times we can witness great revelations, miracles, or blessings from God to then find our selves in the flesh. Moses didn't follow God's instruction after all the miracles and blessings he had. Moses was not allowed to lead the people into the Promised Land. David, Peter, Thomas, Judas, Rebecca, Abraham at times went from a mountain of faith into a flesh reaction or action. It happened to us today.

How foolish.

Or look at the apostle Peter, in Matthew 16. Jesus asks his disciples who others say He is, and then He asks His disciples to tell Him who they think He is. Peter rightly answers that Jesus is the Christ, the Son of the Living God. He gets high praise for this answer from Jesus, who says that God revealed this to Peter. What a great moment of faith.

Until only seconds later, when Jesus makes a comment, Peter tries to rebuke Him, and Jesus calls Him "Satan" and to watch what kind of foolish nonsense comes out of his mouth.

That was quick, right?

But Peter answered foolishly the second time, because Jesus was speaking of His coming death on the cross, and it sounds like that idea worried Peter.

Fear can rush in if we aren't careful, even on the very heels of a faithful act.

We must trust God all of the time.

Fear has another slippery tactic of attacking us only in certain areas of life. For instance, you may have all kinds of faith that God will provide for your financial needs, but as soon as a big problem opens in a relationship, you are filled with fear. Or you might have faith in communing with God privately and seeking Him in prayer every day, but when the Spirit asks you to share about Him to your neighbor, you freeze up.

Isn't this silly? We all do it, but it makes no sense. If God is God when we need money, he's also God when we need to patch things up with our spouses. If God is God when you need to do His work privately, He is still God when you need to do the work publicly.

Moses seemed to struggle with this very thing.

When he saw the burning bush,[7] Moses took off his shoes, worshiped the Lord, and listened to God's voice. He was in communion with God Almighty.

But then God went and asked Him to be in communion with God publicly. He asked Moses to conduct a mission, and all the sudden, Moses was a stuttering, excuse-making guy on the outside of things, as if he hadn't just been chosen by God and put into His presence.

"It's cool to serve you here at the bush, Lord, but now You want me to take this thing public??"

We can be that way, I think. But the God we meet privately is the same we can witness of publicly.

At the end of the day, I think that we are afraid that God isn't going to hold up His end of the bargain.

God said, "Be fruitful and multiply," but we say, "I have to wait and wait and wait to have kids with my spouse, because it's expensive out there." God said, "Do not forsake the assembling together of Christian brothers and sisters," but we say, "A church or Bible study group might hurt me, and I don't need a church to be Christian anyway." God said, "Do not worry about tomorrow," and we say, "I have to worry about tomorrow!"

But God is faithful. We should be too.

Now, for those of you who know a little something about the Bible, you might bring up a fair point to contrast with all of this.

"You're saying the Bible teaches us not to fear, but doesn't the Old Testament say "Fear God" over and over and over? So, which is it? Don't fear? Or fear?"

It's a fair question. As with anything, we can't be overly simplistic with what the Bible teaches. We always need to go in and look at context, see who is speaking to who, and how or if specific verses apply to us. But we certainly are told not to be anxious, and we certainly are told to fear God.

The first part of the answer is this:

The Bible does not say, "Hey, all you people reading this throughout time: Never be afraid of anything, or anyone, for any reason, at any time, whatsoever."

But repeatedly, we see people being instructed not to be worried over not having enough of what they need. We see people being told not to be anxious. We see people being told not to be afraid to face enemies who oppose God, because God is greater.

Don't be anxious, in other words. Do not worry. And do not live your life in a general posture of fear. If a poisonous snake falls on your head during a nature hike, it is not sinful to be afraid for a minute, because that fear is going to give you the reflexes to swat the snake off of your head. But don't live in constant fear of snakes.

The second part of the answer to this objection is this: The fear of the Lord is the beginning of wisdom[8], and that means any rational person ought to fear God rather than smaller, less significant things. This will help you set your priorities straight and learn wisdom.

But why be afraid of God? Isn't God love? How can you love someone you are afraid of?

It's a good question, and I wish people would address it more often, because answering it rightly informs how we approach God and how we live our lives.

Let me give you a metaphor the Bible often uses, and we will compare God to an earthly father, and you and I, we'll compared to children.

When I was a kid, I loved my parents deeply. They knew so much about the world. Dad, being a federal agent, taught us to respect the law and law officers. We were not to speed, run stop signs, etc. Well, as a young driver, I got a ticket. My dad wanted me to go to court, and so we did. When my case came before the judge, I was hoping dad would use his influence to help me out. That did not happen. My father's opening statement was, "As an officer of the court, I want to apologize to his honor and the court that my son broke the law by speeding. I do not expect any special considerations." When my dad sat down, my heart sank. I was prepared for the worst, and then the judge spoke. "Well, I think this young man is going to receive far better punishment than I could give." He dismissed the charges.

I was grounded from driving (and from life) for a month, but I learned a lesson of love that day. My father loved me so much as to go with me to court, tell the truth of the situation, and then make a fair judgement because I was guilty. There were moments of fear from getting the ticket, and later in the courtroom with the judge, but those fear moments were overcome by my father's love on earth. I realize many don't have this, but it reminded me how much my heavenly father loves me. On his throne and in His court, I deserved punishment for my sins, but he dismissed the charges against me thanks to Calvary, where Jesus died.

My mom was the best baker in town, and as a boy I learned where she hid the sugar. I thought it would be better kept in my room under my pillow so I could have some sugar anytime I wanted. Well, my mother came to me to ask where the sugar had gone. I lied and said I did not know. She gave me a spanking and asked again, "Where is the sugar?" Like an idiot, I said I did not know, afraid of getting into more trouble. And I did get into more trouble. I got another spanking. (My Mom did not read Dr. Spock.) This happened three times in a row before I told the truth. My mother knew where the sugar was, because I had failed to remember that my mother made my bed for me. I learned valuable lessons from her: not to lie, sugar under my pillow was not a great idea, and when you mess up, fess up!

My Parents both loved me enough to make sure I knew right from wrong. Yes, they punished me, but they also hugged me, loved me, and provided for my needs. I loved spending time with them. I wasn't afraid of being close to them, I was afraid of disobeying them.

Their discipline was real, reasonable, and quick. If I lied, stole, or rebelled against their instructions, I knew that justice would be swift. I had a healthy respect and fear of those consequences, just like I had a healthy respect for mom and dad as people. I did not fear them the way a battered wife fears an abusive My parents were good parents. But their discipline was no joke. That was where the fear was.

I think it's similar with fearing God.

A pastor and writer named David Hoffman has a good line on this in his book The Fear of the Lord. He says, and I'm paraphrasing, "Fearing God means that you respect the fact as fundamental that there are blessings for obeying God and consequences for disobeying God."

I love God with all of my heart, to the best of my ability. I want to be closer to Him, understand Him better, and spend more time with Him. Also, I am terrified to drift away from Him! I don't want to do that. God is where there is protection, wisdom, blessing, and grace. I don't want to rebel against Him! And hopefully, you don't either.

Some early Christian thinkers have written that sin is disordered love. For example, it's fine to love eating cherry pie, but if you can't be bothered to set your pie down to save a woman who's being mugged right next to you, your loves are out of order. You should love people and their well-being more than cherry pie, obviously.

Fear is similar. Don't fear man more than God. Don't be afraid of crossing your boss such that you cross God. Put your faith in God, and all of those earthly fears that paralyze us can fall to the wayside.

Properly understanding God and fearing Him does not lead to paralysis. All it means is you want to obey Him, and that you run straight to Him when you make a mistake. Next to the Creator of the Universe, the Divine Warrior, the Alpha and the Omega – well, anything else we could fear just shrinks up and becomes puny.

If you follow God (faith), you don't need to be anxious over other things.

Let faith drive out your fear. That is the path God has laid out for us.

A friend of mine at Apison Baptist is Ralph Gwaltney. Being an engineer, he can fix anything... (like my car, my mower, garage door, AC, plumbing). At our church we had a workday and Ralph climbed up a set of ladders on the roof and walked back and forth like I wanted to change the channel to my TV. He has no fear of heights or the danger of a roof needing repairing. Not many people can do that, but Ralph's gifting and faith is not like mine or yours. We all have areas of strengths that might be a weakness for someone else, that is why we unite in a faith community to help one another on our journey of faith. God knows your fears, trust Him!

To paraphrase a writer, I read online a few years ago, "The fear of the Lord is the beginning of wisdom, but it isn't the end."

Love is the destination.

But before we delve into that, we're going to examine how to stay close to Jesus and overcome the fears that assault us during this life.

Fear, at least fear of earthly things, is a liar.

Chapter 11

Following Jesus in the Midst of Fear

One summer night, during a severe and loud thunderstorm, a mother was tucking her small son into bed. She was about to turn the light off when he asked in a trembling voice, "Mommy, will you stay with me all night?" Smiling, the mother gave him a warm, reassuring hug and said tenderly, "I can't dear. I have to sleep in Daddy's room." A long silence followed. At last, it was broken by a shaky voice saying, "That big sissy!"

I found that online somewhere, and it always makes me laugh. It reminds me of when I was a child, afraid of the storms, and my mother tried to comfort me by telling me the angels were bowling.

The truth is, we all get scared sometimes, and like the boy in the joke, we want God to appear visibly before us every second of the day. If we could, most of us would say, "God, you know the right thing to do and I just mess things up. So, you can just do whatever you want. Send me a list of everything I've got to do today."

But He doesn't usually work that way, does He?

God isn't interested in having a bunch of robots work for Him. He's interested in shaping us into the image of His Son Jesus. And Jesus is no robot. He has perfect freedom of will and action, but He chooses only to follow the will of the Father.

That's what He would have from us, too.

Now, that's a tall order, right?

For some, they aren't too keen on following Jesus because it might land them in trouble with the elites of our world. It might mean they raise their families and live their lives in a way that gets funny looks. They're afraid to follow because they fear the opinions of those around them.

For others, they want to follow God, but they fear doing it badly, and, like I mentioned in the previous chapter, fear paralyzes us. It stops us in our tracks.

In either case, if we want to follow Jesus, we're going to need to overcome fear.

And I have some good news if you've messed this up in the past:

You're in good company. God gives second chances.

> *And someone came to Him and said, "Teacher, what good thing shall I do so that I may obtain eternal life?" And He said to him, "Why are you asking Me about what is good? There is only One who is good; but if you want to enter life, keep the commandments." Then he said to Him, "Which ones?" And Jesus said, "You shall not commit murder; You shall not commit adultery; You shall not steal; You shall not give false testimony; Honor your father and mother; and You shall love your neighbor as yourself." The young man said to Him, "All these I have kept; what am I still lacking?" Jesus said to him, "If you want to be complete, go and sell your possessions and give to the poor, and you will have treasure in heaven; and come, follow Me." But when the young man heard this statement, he went away grieving; for he was one who owned much property.*
> – Matthew 19:16-22

Two important things to note here before we really dig in:

1. Jesus' instruction to this young man to sell everything he had was, in fact, specific to the situation.

Sometimes people get weird with this passage, and they claim that owning anything at all is immoral, and that's just silly. Jesus was inviting this young man to be a disciple and accept Him as his rabbi. In ancient Jewish culture, this meant the young man would literally go everywhere that Jesus went, do everything that He did, and spend as much time with him as humanly possible. Keeping a bunch of possessions, in that scenario, would not make a lot of sense. Many faith journeys have never begun because of material and earthly desires that make many walks away grieved for they own much.

SECTION IV: *Conquering the Mountain of Fear*

But in a sense, we do all need to give it all up if we're going to follow Jesus in our lives today. God suffers no rivals, and He is not willing to be #2 in your heart. To follow Jesus, we do need to loosen our grip on everything else, ready to be released at any moment if the Lord asks us to.

2. The nameless young man did not do as Jesus said. He could have been the 13th disciple, but he said No to the direct invitation.

The passage says that "he went away grieving." In the moment, this may have been a failure. After all, such an invitation from Jesus Himself should have been met with joy! He should have been jumping up and down, clicking his heels. Take the world and give me Jesus!

But he failed the heart test at that moment.

Even still, that doesn't mean he was beyond saving, or that God was done with him. Some Bible teachers say that tests in the Bible are not all about passing or failing, but instead that they are about revealing the quality of someone (thus the word Testimony). If you evaluate a rope, you're trying to figure out how strong it is and what you can use it for. It is a little more than pass/fail sometimes.

What this interaction revealed to the rich young man was that his possessions possessed him. The idea of giving them up in exchange for the greatest honor in the world grieved him. He could understand the concept of FAITH living.

This is where the term "golden handcuffs" comes from. Sure, this young man had quite a lot, but those possessions came with strings attached.

He wasn't ready to follow Jesus with gladness.

The good news here is something we don't find in the Bible, but some church tradition tells us that this rich young ruler was named John Mark – the same John Mark that went on to serve with Paul and Barnabas, and the same John Mark that worked with Peter to write the oldest written record of Jesus' activity on earth that we have: The Gospel of Mark. This is a theory but one thing to consider is he frustrated Paul and left the mission field and Barnabas nurtured him, if the same person, you can see he struggled with FAITH living from rich living.

He got it right eventually.

He was scared! He was afraid that if he let go of all of his possessions, he would not be able to acquire them again. Perhaps he was afraid of what might happen to his property and belongings under the ownership of someone else.

He was grieved, and that grief cost him the moment.

But it was a battle, and not the war, and I'm here to tell you today that if you've missed your chance with Jesus in the past, here is another opportunity, right now, wherever you are. You can get it right this time. You can still go and do what He's asking of you.

Even during fear, you can still obey God and follow close. You'll be glad you did.

Money comes and goes. Nice things rust and wear out. Land erodes, floods, declines in value, or, at best, you keep it until you die, and then you lose it by default. But following Jesus bears fruit that echoes into eternity.

Have you ever noticed some that purchase clothing, shoes, cars, or other possessions for the name brand, because they feel like it will brand them with that company's worldly success? The brand of Jesus was paid for with the rich, royal blood of Jesus, and if you can see past the material and into the eternal... Well, that is the best brand of all: a child of the King that has no fear or failure.

Many use so many grooming products, skin care, tanning, cosmetics, and spend hours a day getting ready to interact with humans, many they do not even know. Then when it comes to getting ready to pray to an almighty God, we spend seconds in preparation and participation. The bible tells us He is a jealous God.

If we fear God and regard Him over the concerns of this world, then we will see that gaining Christ is worth losing everything else. If we fear God, we don't need to fear anything else.

Following Jesus has that effect on people. We see it with the apostle Peter in the Bible.

Now, Peter could be somewhat brash, but that isn't the same thing as brave. Before Jesus' crucifixion, he denied Christ three separate times. Why? Because he was afraid. He let that fear led him to denying association with the very man that he had left everything to follow.

Fear makes us act in ways that don't make any sense.

SECTION IV: *Conquering the Mountain of Fear*

But after Jesus' resurrection, Jesus forgave Peter, and He gave Peter the Holy Spirit. We can read about what Peter did after Jesus' ascension into heaven, and, wow, what a difference.

Peter became a lion.

In the face of social shaming, government coercion, physical violence, difficulties, and death itself, Peter followed Jesus fearlessly.

When you realize that all this isn't just some song and dance, and that the One who is asking you to follow is really God Almighty, your heart changes.

For believers in certain parts of the world today, it isn't slight social ramifications that have people afraid to follow Jesus, it is actual, real persecution. People have been thrown in jail and killed for Christ's sake, but as they walked through heaven's pearly gates, they saw Jesus standing at the right hand of the throne of the Father, saying, "Well done."

We have to get our fears in order. We have to prioritize our love.

> *"For what good will it do a person if he gains the whole world, but forfeits his soul? Or what will a person give in exchange for his soul?"*
>
> – Jesus, Matthew 16:26

It all comes down to one simple question, no matter what fear is telling you to worry about: do you trust Jesus?

If you do, following Him is worth any price.

And remember too – fear is a liar. Oftentimes, what we're worried about doesn't even happen at all. We might be afraid a friend will cut us out if we share Christ, and then it turns out they are receptive to the gospel. Suddenly, when you've gained a soul for the kingdom instead of losing a friend, those fears seem pretty silly.

But even when our worries do really happen, our faith reminds us that God will judge, and we can trust in His promises.

It's for this reason that we all need a community of Christian brothers and sisters around us. Fear multiplies when we are isolated, but when you confess your sins to others (not just in your prayers), when you worship together, encourage each other, and strengthen each other in the truth of the Scriptures, your faith grows.

I'm convinced that the apostle Thomas would have left the path if not for the other apostles. "Doubting Thomas" didn't believe that Jesus had really raised from the dead until He saw Jesus appear in their midst. But if he had not continued in fellowship with those other men who stayed committed, would he have been able to see the resurrected Christ? Over time, would his doubts and fears have turned into a faith disaster?

Fear + doubt = disaster, at least it does if you do not share your burdens with other believers around you, who can help lift you up when you are vulnerable and weak. It is for our blessing, as well as for the good of our world, that the Bible commands us to not forsake the assembly of faith.

> *Not forsaking the assembling of ourselves together, as the manner of some is but exhorting one another: and so much the more, as ye see the day approaching.*
>
> – Hebrews 10:25

Many have bad opinions of the organized church, denominations, and certain faith gatherings. The bible is calling for us to unite with fellow bible faith believers, not become a denomination loyalist, just don't be a lone ranger believer.

> *As iron sharpens iron, so one person sharpens another.*
>
> – Proverbs 27:17

> Macilism: "Some people say that you can be a Christian without the church. I say, it's awfully difficult for a coal to stay hot if you take it out of the fire pit."

You don't have to be in a bubble, and I think it's a good thing to have friends and associates who are not believers – otherwise, who are you preaching the good news to? But make sure you are part of a thriving Christian community. You need them. And they might just need you too.

My friend and fitness trainer Bobby Parker is a retired marine. He is a featured guest on my radio show each Monday, "Monday Muscle with Bobby and Josh Kilgore." Bobby's testimony is that he became an alcoholic while serving in Afganastan. He was a functional drinker if you will but after his tours were up, he came to the stateside and they would not re-enlist him for the anger

SECTION IV: *Conquering the Mountain of Fear*

and issues he developed serving our nation in a dark part of the world at the time. His wife Kami, a solid Christian prayed for him all this time. He hit rock bottom and a large church in town Bayside Baptist led him the Christ and he was baptized. I have watched Bobby these past two years grow. He is now a part of a house church reaching out to men like him that were outside the kingdom. I share this to say we need all sizes of churches. Bayside offered him things and his family that blessed them, and they poured into his family and now he is a lay missionary pouring into other families. His Iron of faith is sharpening others, even mine at times. We must all find a faith family to share our faith journey with and share our giftings and talents so we can punch a hole in hell!

Jesus is asking you to follow Him today, whether you've never said yes to God before, or if today is just another adventure on the path of faith. You are left with two questions:

1. What does following Jesus today look like?
2. What is preventing me from tossing my fears aside?

The first one is something that we should all meditate on daily. We must search the scriptures every day for fresh inspiration and instruction. It is all too easy to rely on that dose of faith you got thirty years ago at VBS, but God is asking you to seek Him out today. It's a new day, and that new day needs new direction. Don't put old wine in new wineskins.

Jesus said that the greatest commandment was to love the Lord with all your heart, soul, and mind. He said that the second greatest commandment was to love others as yourself.

Everything else is going to come back to these two things.

Love God.

Love others.

If you do this, you will be following Jesus – but here's the catch. God gets to define what "loving" looks like.

Read the Bible, seek out wise instruction, and pray to God to learn how to love Him and the people He created. Some of this is intuitive, and some of it isn't. But there are answers if we keep seeking and knocking.

The second question is something only you can answer.

What fears keep you from following Jesus, if any?

And why don't you forsake those fears in favor of a closer walk with Christ? I've had days were worrying over money was keeping me from following Jesus. When I was in full time evangelism and traveling around the country doing revivals and bible conferences it was a lot of fun but at times the love offerings or checks were not enough. I seriously prayed over our mailbox one time. We had little groceries and with three little girls and a wife you feel the weight of provision. God always provided for us.

The Holy Spirit wanted to speak to me, comfort me, and guide me, but I was crowding Him out by dwelling on a financial problem I didn't know how to solve and letting myself grow anxious over it. But following Jesus on those days meant trusting what God says in the Scriptures, that He would provide for my needs if I sought Him first. I had to trust Him, and that mountain of fear crumbled to the ground.

I've had times when a fear of failure was keeping me from following Jesus. He was asking me to step out boldly, but I was afraid that God wouldn't support my efforts, and that I'd fall flat on my face. But following Jesus on those days meant believing that 'where God guides, He provides,' and embracing the idea that being obedient to Jesus is worth making a fool of myself or coming up short. I had to trust in the surpassing worth of Christ, and that mountain of fear crumbled to the ground.

"Do not be afraid," "Fear Not" the Bible says repeatedly. Sometimes it is saying, "Do not be afraid of opposition," other times it is saying, "Do not be afraid to speak the truth," or "Do not be afraid for your life."

The mountain of fear looms large when it rises in front of us. But keep walking ahead, trusting God, and you'll find that the mountain was just a hologram.

Fear is a liar. God is trustworthy.

I urge you to say "yes" to Him today.

Chapter 12

Faith Is Fueled by Provision

It was another Friday evening. All the people that rely on our food pantry for daily provisions had been fed and supplied. No one had gone home empty handed. And yet, as I stared at those bare shelves, part of me had to wonder how on earth we were going to do it again next week.

It is a small miracle that we witness weekly. Linda, our Treasure, and record keeper will tell you that we weigh in thousands of pounds of food each week that is donated or bought, and within days, it is given away. She is a retired math teacher, and I don't know what we would do without her.

Janet, our director, is a combination of Martha and Mary, she works so very hard, and nobody can match her pace and yet she has such a kind heart for the clients and people in need. Many times, Janet and Linda sacrifice family time, personal finances and resources so that hungry people can have food.

Imogene, Mary, Julie, Jill and my wife Judy are in leadership roles that we cannot make unless each one carries their weight. We have Methodist, Baptist, Lutheran, Nazarene, Church of God, Catholic, Adventist, Non-Denominational churches plus local bible studies/small groups all working together to organize this miracle in Jesus' name each week.

Words cannot express the joy it brings me to pastor a ministry that enjoys helping others so much. This little miracle each week makes me smile. No matter how unlikely it seems, God provides for this ministry, and we keep serving our community. Every week, our shelves fill up just in time.

One special lady that got me to work at the pantry is Mrs. Anette Gwaltney. She is 89 at the writing of this book and gets to the pantry every Friday at

9 am and stays we close around 3:30 pm and every client knows her. She is our Jesus in the flesh happy face that greets each car as it arrives and helps answer questions. But six years earlier, I was a new pastor at Apison. Praying and fasting for God to open a door to help this church get on track.

Annettee kept inviting me to come help load boxes. Well, I thought I should go check it out and maybe I could get this lady satisfied if I went to help them. After a few times helping the Lord kept prompting me to get more involved. I went to help more, they asked me to serve on the board, then after a year they asked if our church would take it over. Now we rent two old grocery stores, have bought four commercial freezers and five commercial refrigerators, a delivery van and we feed thousands a month. Thanks to a sweet lady, retired from earthly work but not heavenly. You just might be an Annette to others. Looking back over these past six years to see the growth and blessings is truly a God thing. Annette will always be dear to my heart for inviting me over and over to come load boxes, it changed my life and our churches!

The homeless downtown call me "Preacher man in the white van." There is a local store manager that is a professed agnostic and non-church goer that can never remember my name or the churches but calls us "That church that feeds the hungry." God has allowed us the spiritual face lift we prayed for to help our church become a salt and light base for our community.

When we took over the food pantry, it had a little over three hundred families in the computer registry. Since then, we have more than tripled the number of families we serve and workers that volunteer. We give out food every Friday for five hours to hundreds of families each week. At 3 pm when we shut down, the shelves, freezers, and refrigerators are empty or empty as we give out 4-5 thousand pounds of food.

Then, through food drives, donations, and bulk purchasing, we witness that small miracle of how God provides just enough to feed families week to week.

We are now open seven days a week for donations, pick up in our van, we weigh all food that comes in, stock it on a shelf, or place it in a cooler or freezer. Each day we have a volunteer team that believes in our cause and performs these tasks so that we are ready to feed the hungry each Friday. We like to give each family a large box of food, a box of fresh vegetables, dessert, bread, and meat.

Thanks to small groups, neighborhood food drives, local police in Collegedale, faith groups like Salt and Light, local gardens and farms... it is always just enough for that week.

Just recently, our food pantry ran completely out of canned goods, and we needed them. We prayed – Janet, Linda, Imogene, Jill, Judy, and me.

And would you not know it, I got a phone call from a manager at a local food city. He had 3,000lbs of canned goods that he wanted to donate to us.

That was incredible! But it was not the whole amount that we needed. So, having prayed, we acted. I put a post on Facebook asking people if they could help make up the difference in what we needed. Sure enough, a man pulled up with a massive load of canned goods, five hundred plus pounds! Turns out, he was quite a prepper, and his daughter leaned on him to not let his preparation turn into hoarding. So, he gave the food to the hungry, and the need was met.

My friend from High School, Susan Foster goes to a large church in the area and many times has brought us food, supplies, helped work events, does the little things like vacuum, and carry out the garbage. Susan and her husband are special to me for they have adopted kids, feed the hungry and on many occasions do the little things that only God or the leader would notice. She can't volunteer at the pantry because she lives in Georgia, but she gathers items and then lets me know she is coming with a suburban packed with blessings. We all can do something like Susan even if it is not every week. Pray about it.

My Harley riding friend Greg Gilbert "Mr. Honey" (his wife calls him that) and Marian are big seasonal helpers like Susan. Many times, Marian brings us extra veggies from her garden. They get others to give as well.

Chet Carney, retired Fireman, and lifelong friend helps us out a lot as well. Chet "The Human Forklift" because at age 70 still hits the gym, helps us on many occasions with special pickups, stacking boxes and kind donations. He also has a carpet business. He saw the bad flooring in our office and chapel and replaced it all as a gift. The trivial things add up and Chet is a good friend.

Charlene Nunnery is a new member to our church with an amazing story. As a widow she felt and needed to consolidate and move into the Chattanooga area. She read about our Food pantry in the Baptist and Reflector. She came to help us feed the hungry. Then she started visiting our church. Next thing you know, she buys a home in Apison and is more than a faithful member of the church but also is a faithful worker at the pantry each week. The sense of family we have at the pantry and our church is brining us some very kindred spirits of service for Jesus.

We have seen these kinds of things happen repeatedly, and all I can say is that God is good. Witnessing these people as a pastor impacts my faith.

Right as Covid was about to shut down the globe the medical community had some kind of heads up it seemed. My wife worked in Home Health Care as the head of Human Resources. Suddenly, they let all the HR's go, many other employees on a major scale down. What made this interesting is Judy's job was hiring and firing, they were always behind in workers, and it was difficult to fill schedules due to lack of workers and the high demand of home health care... then a major cut back of employees and the hire fire people? Well Judy got called in that her job was being terminated. There goes our insurance and income, you start asking God why us? Then looking back, we realize why.

Judy is not able to sit still, she is a diligent worker, planner, and the ultimate Martha in the bible. We had just taken over the food pantry officially a few weeks earlier and the change over was not a smooth one at first. We had people that were taking things and not being honest. We tried one lady that was not a church member as director, and it was a major failure.

Then when Janet agreed to serve, Judy had just lost her job and jumped right in. I honestly believe Judy kept the pantry from having a major setback at the time of transition. Some of the inherited people were giving Janet a tough time. One lady even in the chapel service tried to call Janet out as I was giving a devotion. Janet's crime? Making everyone get the same amount and document... they were not use to that. Judy, being a lady, could say things I could not to some of the fellow workers.

We had just been given a van for pickups. One of my former youth, Jeremy, from First Baptist Cary, NC sent a check. A friend from high school Marcus Moore paid to have new tires put on, then Bill Hullander paid to have our logo painted on both sides.

Judy took over the driver rotations, insurance, and driver's license with our insurance. Lining up drivers daily is no easy task. Plus, she helped Janet with her plan to restructure the layout of food storage and distribution. Those 18 months Judy was out of work were tough on us financially, but it was a blessing to work side by side with my wife daily feeding the hungry. Covid ended and then Judy got an incredible job that she loves, we got health insurance again and have about caught up on that eighteen-month gap, but the Lord always provides.

On a side note, giving God glory. Judy had a medical procedure that needed to be done and was scheduled for outpatient surgery. When she lost her job, she called to cancel. Then somehow, we were given a huge help from the hospital that paid for her surgery, more so than if she had her old insurance. God will never let us down when we remain faithful.

One of the biggest ways that the mountain of fear stands in our way, is by threatening us with not having the things that we need to be successful. It could be money, courage, skill, or opportunity – whatever we need, we can fear not having it when it is needed. But on the other side, every time we see God come through, that mountain of fear gets a little bit smaller. If God did it last time, why wouldn't He do it again? If my needs were met before, back when it seemed so impossible, why can't it happen again?

Fear can paralyze us if we allow it to dominate our lives. But remembering the times we have been provided for builds our faith. Praying with our faith family in times of need and sharing scripture together also is a fear buster.

When I was pastoring a church in Charlotte, years ago, I was distressed by a debt that the church owed by the leadership before I came. We needed to pay it off to also try and clam the dissention the leaders had among themselves. I challenged our congregation to take ownership, and to split the debt evenly among every member of the church. It came out to around $200 per person, that I was asking people to pledge to give over and above their tithes.

Fine, but this included me as well, and as the primary breadwinner in my family, it meant I was on the hook to pay for five people's shares. I did not have an extra $1,000 laying around, so I prayed. I made the pledge, and I made the first payment that I could.

Something funny started happening then. I got checks in the mail.

The first was a refund check from Verizon. They had overcharged me in the past, and they sent me back $200. I had never gotten a refund check from Verizon before or since. I said a prayer of thanks and paid off another chunk of the debt at church.

Then I got another refund check – this time from the power company. Who ever heard of a refund check from the power company? I sure had not gotten one before. Then another bonus check came to us from another company. Now $600 in refunds may not sound like a lot to you but a preacher with three girls and a wife that was huge. A member of my church told me that they wanted to pay me a bonus, and so I took that money and paid off my pledge.

It is all God's money anyway, but since I responded with faith instead of fear, my family and I got to be part of paying off that debt in the church.

When we give sacrificially, God provides abundantly. I believe that. I have witnessed that. And why should that be?

God is a giver. Look at the first few words of John 3:16 –

For God so loved the world that He gave...

You cannot outgive God. He loves to give back.

This is not name it and claim it. I am not telling you that the blessings you receive back will always be financial in nature. Many donate online to help our food pantry by going to www.ApisonBaptist.com.

Some will not like that I have started talking about money but understand that if you walk the path of faith, which means you trust God with everything. Yes, even your finances. Giving is a matter of the heart. It must be of free will. Let it be an offering to God.

At Apison Baptist Church, we take four mission's offerings per year, we do a fundraiser for the food pantry and for Operation Christmas Child, and we take at least two offerings for the Gideons (the people who leave Bibles in hotel rooms). That is 8 love offerings from our little church, in addition to normal tithes. I understand that this is difficult – overhead is expensive, these days finances change like the wind with our banking system.

Bottom line is that we are givers not just takers in the Kingdom of God. In the gospels, Jesus fed the four thousand with only seven loaves and a few fish. In His hands, which was more than enough, and there was plenty left over!

And they all ate and were satisfied, and they picked up what was left over of the broken pieces, seven large baskets full. And those who ate were four thousand men, besides women and children.
– Matthew 15:37-38

I find it a significant coincidence that we feed thousands of people a month at the food pantry and homeless ministry now. It is a reminder to me that God has done this sort of thing before – and with much less!

Only a year after taking over the food pantry, COVID hit, and all of the sudden everyone was shutting down. We looked at each other, prayed hard, and decided, "We can't stop doing the Lord's work." We stayed open! We were the only food distribution service in the city to stay open for several weeks, so all of the sudden, in a resource crunch, we now had far more people to feed. Our faith got stretched and strengthened!

We were determined not to let fear get the best of us, and you should not either – no matter what you're facing. We watched most of the world and in our area all the churches and food ministries stopped, staying open was our time to shine.

Instead of just the local Apison community, all the sudden we had families coming from Soddy-Daisy, Cleveland, Red Bank, White Oak, North Georgia, and other towns nearby. But we also started getting calls from restaurants we had never worked with before, because they were looking for whoever was open. And in the moment of crisis, we were open. As I said earlier and told our people, "It was our time to shine in a dark time."

Restaurants like St. Johns, 1885, and Five Guys Burger told us, "They are closing us down. Can you folks take our food?" And we would say yes. We gave it all away.

We rented two old grocery stores. We inherited twenty-seven old refrigerators. Each week we would have just enough. Then we would prepare for the small miracle of gathering enough food again.

Some pastors rebuked me for keeping the church and the food pantry open. Also, that I am a non-vaxer some bought into the Ouchie Fauci hype that has now been proven untrue. I just said, "It is our time to shine in a dark situation." Later a large church pastor called to tell me he regretted taking the shots and shutting his church down. People need to be able to take a vaccination or not without being condemned.

Strangely, staying open during COVID put us on the map. As we were faithful, the blessings kept pouring in.

A man approached me and said that he would like to donate his piano to our church. It was a white grand piano! It matched our fellowship hall perfectly. We love singing and worshiping along with that wonderful instrument. It appraised for over $14,500 with ivory keys. The reasons he gave it, he was impressed that we did not comply or cower, and he said if we worshipped on Saturdays he would come to our church.

The bottom line is our time on this planet is limited. We will all die someday. In time most of us will be forgotten. As a Christian we are to be Kingdom focused. Twenty or fifty years from now Macil Duncan will not be remembered but if I pant seeds and share the gospel, Jesus' work will. That's our goal, plant faith seeds to grow to impact others faith for generations to come.

Another faith story. We got a call from Party City one time, as the holidays were drawing near. During this global supply chain crisis caused by the lockdowns, ships at sea not docking, their store had gotten a double shipment. (Think about that, re-read that sentence). They had no storage space to accommodate all the stuff – they literally had boxes filling all of their aisleways, and naturally, with it still being COVID, they weren't doing the sort of business they were used to. They asked us if we wanted a big load of party supply store stuff. What is funny is, we'd just been praying that the Lord would fill our supply closet with things to bless others with, and we were filling boxes for Operation Christmas Child (like Toys for Tots) anyway. We got a few truckloads delivered to us. Our Christmas boxes were filled and sent out, we gave tons of the stuff to other churches, and our supply closet was filled.

On another occasion, a man named David Tullis came to visit us, having heard about our ministry. He introduced himself after service at our church, and he told me that he had a show on the local radio station. He asked if I would not mind being a guest sometime. I said yes, and the show went well, and eventually it led to me having my own show once a week. Later, that became five days a week during drive-home traffic, carried by a small network of radio stations across several states. Today, I am blessed to be able to speak to thousands of listeners live on the radio and on social media replays. Why? Because we did not shut down.

If we are faithful in the trivial things, God will bless us with greater things that we never asked for and never could have imagined. I try to remember that Jesus told us to be two things: Salt (which is a preservative) and light (to repel

SECTION IV: *Conquering the Mountain of Fear*

darkness). Next time a tragedy or trial happens in your neighborhood, remember that you can meet it with faith instead of fear. Because maybe that will be your time to shine.

And each time you respond in faith, you get to see how He miraculously provides.

In our second year of running the food pantry, I thought it would be nice if we could give a turkey away to each family. Now, that is a lot of money when you multiply it out, and it didn't seem feasible. But we prayed.

At our executive team meeting, I said that it was my prayer that we would be able to give each family a turkey this year. One of the ladies smiled ironically and said, "Pastor, we are not there yet. I just do not see that happening."

But sure enough, the next day my phone rang. It was an accounting firm. The person on the other line said, "Pastor, we do a turkey drive every year, and we have an organization that we usually give them to, but I heard about what you are doing. Anyway, can we give you all 69 Butterball turkeys?"

I gratefully accepted.

Two days after that, I got a call from a local grocery store. The assistant manager there told me, "Listen, because you are not going to believe this. My store manager told me to 'call that church that feeds the hungry and give him these five turkeys.'"

I thought his level of excitement was a little out of order for the size of the donation, but I said OK, and I took the van out to pick up five turkeys.

As it turns out, I had misheard him. It was 5,000 pounds of turkey and assorted meats. My arms had turned to jelly by the time I was finished loading the van, so I texted our group of volunteers for help with the unloading. By the time I got back to the pantry, Mary our Methodist champion had ten people to lend a hand. We had to unload, weigh it all in, then fill every freezer at the pantry and the church.

What made this a special story is my friend Matt Hullander donated two new commercial freezers. One of them was never plugged in because some did not believe we could fill it. Sadly, a little lack of faith sends us scrambling for freezer space, but it all worked out. We learned to ask in faith and if it is His will it will happen, feeding the hunger is His will friend.

We came to a point when we needed more space to rent. God provided Bill Hullander – our landlord, a deacon, community leader, and friend. Bill has even driven the van to do food pick-ups, and his son Matt, another community leader and friend, has helped us out as well. Bill is one of those that will truly pray for you and his wife Linda are salt of the earth people. The people of Apison call him "Mayor Bill" because he just knows who to call to get problems solved.

During Covid Bill Hullander, Senator Todd Gardenhire, The "ROOF DOCTOR" Greg Bolton, Chet Carney, and others helped me do a Facebook live fund raiser and we raised over $30,000 for the Food Pantry that November-December.

Once the Tennessee legislature opened, Senator Gardenhire had me come to the first opening prayer of the Tennessee Senate. That was an honor and blessing. He shared with them how we feed the hungry. I asked them if for just a few minutes could we not be a Republican or a Democrat, just Americans? I prayed for God to bless them and their families and honor their hearts. After a 3-4-minute prayer they all stood and applauded, five canes and gave me a hug. I went to the back and asked if I could take a selfie and the guard at the door said after that prayer you can take as many as you like. I did not understand. He then went on to say many people come and pray at them or rebuke them, he said you loved them, and they do not get that often. He said, "take all the pictures you want preacher." It was then I realized these people are like you and me, tender and in need of encouragement at times. We most certainly do not agree on everything, but we can learn to love others that believe differently from us.

As we have been blessed, we try to also be a blessing to others. From time to time, we even have enough food donations to share with other organizations. Once, while my friend David and I were driving down to minister to the homeless, the Lord laid the Chattanooga community soup kitchen on my heart. So, David and I stopped by the pantry and loaded up a large stack of snack cakes, then headed off to the soup kitchen. As we walked through the door, I asked if they could use some snack cakes, and the guy in charge just looked at me. After a moment, he turned around and yelled, "Problem solved!" and gladly accepted our donation. Turns out, they had just run out of desserts, and they had been praying for something to give the homeless to go with their meal. It was, in his words, "perfect timing."

God's timing always is.

I could tell you all sorts of stories. I could even go on and on about the food pantry. That would say nothing of the ministry we have for the homeless, the "Janet Bags" we give away (full of needed supplies like toilet paper, socks, protein bars, food, and a New Testament). Janet, our Pantry Director produced using a gallon zip lock bag to hand out supplies to the homeless. I go downtown to tent cities and veterans sleeping on the streets to share Jesus and supplies with the help of the Gideons. We led a 75-year-old man to Jesus and he and the Gideon both wept at the tent city as the man had always wanted to know how to have a relationship with God. Many times, I drive home with leaky eyes after helping the homeless and hungry in my local area. My friend Sabrina Smedley, our District 7 Commissioner at time went down and she just wept and said I had no idea we had so many hungry people.

Our mayor Tim Kelley has designated land downtown now for a tent city with fencing so at night the ladies feel protected. They have a kitchen tent and we have provided them with two refrigerators, oven, toaster, walkie talkies, and lots of other supplies and food. The mayor is not a conservative GOP, but we work together because he has a heart. Politicians at times do let us down, anger us but if we look closely and try to be kind, we can find good efforts in most of them. That is why every Thanksgiving we have a community meal to raise funds for the pantry but also to invite all elected officials to be prayed over and reminded that we appreciate them. Congressman Chuck Flashman, Senator Todd Gardenhire, Tennessee Rep Greg Vital, public servants Marty Hanes, Lee Helton, Jeff Eversole, Police Chief Jack Sapp, and many others come by

Feeding the hungry takes funding and food drives. I am amazed at time how the Lord does it. "Where God guides, He always provides." Every year I grow older, I grow more confident that God is going to come through. You can bet on His promises. You can be confident that He will not leave you hanging when you partner with him. It might not always look like what you expected, but if you keep an open heart, open hands, with just a little bit of tenacity and a tiny drop of faith, wonderful things can happen.

And the fear just sort of fades away.

It is alright if you feel fear on occasion as you step out to do the Lord's work. But let each time the Lord comes through chip away at that fear. Let it go from being a mountain, to a pebble. Eventually, that fear will be nothing at all. The journey of faith will take you up to your fears – I promise you that! But be strong and of good courage, just like the Lord told Joshua in the Old Testament. Because if the Lord is fighting for you, who can stand against you?

God certainly is not afraid. So why should we be? Faith conquers fear. My final tip on dealing with fear is to try and have a prayer partner, someone you can trust your inner heart with. Do not just talk to each other, take time to talk to God together. The bible promises…

Jesus said,

> *"Where two or more are gathered in my name there will I be also."*
> – Matthew 18:20.

Section IV: Summary

Conquering the Mountain of Fear

- Fear is a liar.

- Only God is worthy of fear.

- Fearing God means recognizing that there are blessings for obeying Him and consequences for disobeying Him. You can fear God and love Him at the same time.

- God does not want us to fear anything, ultimately, that is lesser than Him.

- Tests, even when we fail them, are helpful for determining what is in our hearts.

- God gives second chances.

- Being involved in a community of believers can help us overcome our fears.

- Following Jesus will require you to face your fears.

- Everyone has resource-related fears at some point. But as you see God provide, that fear should grow smaller over time.

- Remember the times God has come through for you.

Epilogue

Love Is the Destination

When I was right out of seminary, pastoring my first church plant, I got to witness something extraordinary.

We were meeting in a public library, and we would always give time to prayer at the end of service. Marsha brought her husband, Joe (a rough Truck Driver), to me, and their daughter was with them as well. They had been praying for him to receive salvation, and now – here he was.

But that was not all. He told me he had a lump on the back of his neck that had just been tested. It was cancer. No one ever wants to hear, "It's cancer," and I could see how the devastating news was affecting him and his family.

I asked Joe if he knew Jesus as his Lord and Savior. He said that he had his doubts, but his daughter, Samantha had explained God's plan of salvation to him. In tears, he explained that God had gotten a hold of him, and he now believed in Jesus with all his heart.

Joe's wife had told him that the book of James says that the sick ought to come to the elders of the church, be anointed with oil, and receive prayer for healing. I had never prayed in this way before, but a new member of our church had recently given me a bottle of oil, so I took it and anointed him with it. Then, we prayed.

The next day, at a checkup, his doctor looked at him funny.

"Where is your lump?" he asked.

"It's right here, behind this ear," Joe started to say, but as he reached for it, he realized that it was gone.

His cancer simply... left.

Now, why would God choose to do something like that for this man? His child like faith that brought a tough truck driver to a new church plant and young preacher in his mid-twenty's meeting in a public library. When I reflect on that day I get God-bumps down my arms. But what I know for sure, is that God healed that man.

He did it for love.

In 1 Corinthians 13, the apostle Paul writes a beautiful, flowing discourse on the nature of love. He compares it with prophecy, with knowledge; he explains what love is and is not. He talks about the heights, the depths, the rulers of this world, and all things great and small. But at the end of his discourse, he says this:

> *But now faith, hope, and love remain, these three; but the greatest of these is love.*
>
> – 1 Corinthians 14:13

As we prepare to close this book, that is what I would like to leave you with. The journey of faith is beautiful, necessary, and valuable, but let us never forget that it is taking us someplace.

Love is the destination.

Love is the end of all faith.

Love is the reason for our hope.

Love is the meaning of it all.

Whatever you do, whether you are facing down a mountain of bitterness, a tower of division, or a great big dose of fear, let faith in Jesus guide you through it. Remember always, even in that, that love lies waiting at the end.

Knowledge is crucial, but it is not enough.

Personal moral uprightness is good, but it cannot save you.

Generosity, wisdom, and power all have their limitations, and in the end, even all the faith in the world is worthless if we do not have this one, all-important thing: Love.

My friend Joe, who was healed of the cancer, went home, and made me a prayer bench that is in my office to this day. 30 years later, I still use it. He brought his family to visit me at Apison Baptist and wanted his three grandsons to meet the pastor that prayed over him, and to see the prayer bench in my office. The love of God changed his life, and he loves to give God all the glory for healing him.

We all have cancer/sin infection in our life. Healing is best received in the love that only God can provide. Be blessed my friend and may your journey of faith infect others with the love of Christ!

My mother is one of the most loving people I know. As a child her kiss could heal any hurt and her hugs could take away the pains of the world. Even to this day, Barbra love is as close to Jesus for me for she prays for me and others so much. Take her love times a million and that is not even close to the Love God has for us. Just remember that His love for you and others is literally beyond measure. That is why we must share the gospel of Jesus Christ to all that will listen.

Not everyone has a Barbra momma like me. Some may have never had anyone really love them so to hear a God loves them may sound odd. Our love needs to be as close to Jesus as we can. We must fight through religious, political, social trends and other things that can divide us to love others. It's ok to have convictions, standards, and principles. Just be as loving as possible for the sake of the lost.

> *Beloved, let's love one another; for love is from God, and everyone who loves has been born of God and knows God. The one who does not love does not know God, because God is love. ...We love because God first loved us.*
>
> – 1 John 4:7-8, 19

About the Author

Macil Duncan

Rev. Macil Duncan calls Chattanooga his hometown and finished his elementary, middle and high school education there. He went on to East Tennessee State University to double major in Sociology and Speech Communications. He then went to Mid America Seminary in Memphis to receive his Masters of Divinity degree. He served 20 years as a Student/Small Groups Minister in churches in MS, TX, NC and TN during that time. He served as a Senior Pastor for the past 24 years in NC and TN. Currently Macil is lead pastor at Apison Baptist that also has a 7 day a week Food Pantry that is feeding thousands a month. He also coordinates a Homeless Ministry to those on the streets and tent cities around the Chattanooga area. For the past three years he has hosted a daily radio show on The NOOGA Network broadcasting into TN, GA, AL ,KY and NJ plus on social media platforms like Facebook, Rumble, Truth Social and Telegram. He is married to Judy and they have three daughters; Shaina, Rachel and Maci that are married to godly men that are like sons to them. During the pandemic we did not shut down our church or the food pantry. We felt like this was our time to shine in a dark moment for the world. Feeding the hungry, sharing the gospel and equipping the saints is our goal. Our purpose statement is "Taking Jesus as He is to people as they are." Macil's goal is not to have the largest assembly on Sundays but to be the largest hug of Jesus they can be in the highway and byways to compel them to come to Him. This book is about his faith journey in good and bad times of his ministry. May it bless you to want to increase your faith and serve God and others more now than ever. If you would like to book Macil for speaking engagements or donate to his Zelle or Venmo account to help him with hid broadcasting, help buy materials, supplies to help others, go to ***ChampionshipMinistries@gmail.com***

Authors' Point of Contact

Macil Duncan

- www.macilduncanbooks.com

- champsionshipministries@gmail.com

- @patriotpastormacil

- @macil.duncan

- @macilduncan

- @patriotpastor

Endnotes

1 Try reading through Psalm 119 in one setting and just take note of all the meanings and references to God's Word. It is a good and beneficial exercise.

2 Πίστις, in the Greek

3 שְׁמַע, , or "shema" in Hebrew

4 Marriage and divorce are a large and touchy subject, and, yes, there are sometimes legitimate reasons for divorce. But being unhappy is not one of them.

5 If you are unfamiliar with this reference or the story behind it, read Matthew 26 in the Bible.

6 You can read this story in 1 Kings 18

7 Read this story in Exodus 3.

8 Proverbs 9:10

"Scripture taken from the NEW AMERICAN STANDARD BIBLE,

Copyright © 1960, 1962, 1963 1968, 1971, 1972,
1973 1975, 1977, 1995 by The Lockman Foundation
All rights reserved
Used by permission.
http://www.Lockman.org

When quotations from the NASB® text are used in not-for-sale media, such as church bulletins, orders of service, posters, transparencies or similar media,t he abbreviation (NASB) may be used at the end of the quotation.

This permission is limited to material which is wholly manufactured in compliance witht he provisions of the copyright laws of the United States of America and all applicable international conventions and treaties.

Quotations and reprints in excess of the above limitiations, or other permission requests, must be directed to and approved in writing by The Lockman Foundation, PO Box 2279, La Habra, CA 90632-2279 (714)879- 3055. http://www.lockman.org

www.ingramcontent.com/pod-product-compliance
Lightning Source LLC
Chambersburg PA
CBHW050322120526
44592CB00014B/2011